BEYOND THE BLOCKS

Quilts with Great Borders

NANCY J. MARTIN

Martingale™
& COMPANY

Credits

President . . . . NANCY J. MARTIN
CEO . . . . DANIEL J. MARTIN
Publisher . . . . JANE HAMADA
Editorial Director . . . . MARY V. GREEN
Managing Editor . . . . TINA COOK
Technical Editor . . . . URSULA REIKES
Copy Editor . . . . LIZ MCGEHEE
Design Director . . . . STAN GREEN
Illustrator . . . . LAUREL STRAND
Cover and Text Designer . . . . . . TRINA STAHL
Photographer . . . . BRENT KANE

That Patchwork Place® is an imprint of
Martingale & Company™.

Beyond the Blocks: Quilts with Great Borders
© 2002 by Nancy J. Martin

Martingale & Company
20205 144th Avenue NE
Woodinville, WA 98072-8478 USA
www.martingale-pub.com

ACKNOWLEDGMENTS

Many thanks to the following people:
Beth Kovich, for use of her embroidered blocks in "Stars in the Barnyard"; Kristin Adams, for the use of "Kristin's Stars"; Cleo Nolette, for help in piecing and binding; Alvina Nelson, for her lovely hand quilting and creative quilting designs; Bev Payne, for quilting "Dolly Madison's Amish Star"; Frankie Schmitt, for machine quilting; and Millicent Agnor, for her Amish quilting service and the women who work with her, especially Edna Borntreger, Mary Christner, Wynona Harrington, Mary and Mattie Mast, Mrs. Menno Miller, Lavina Schwartz, Anna Stutzman, Clara Yoder, Mrs. Edward Yoder, and Mrs. Roy M. Yoder

Printed in Hong Kong
07 06 05 04 03 02   8 7 6 5 4 3 2 1

Library of Congress Cataloging-in-Publication Data

Martin, Nancy J.
     Beyond the blocks : quilts with great borders / Nancy J. Martin.
        p. cm.
     ISBN 1-56477-444-9
1. Quilting—Patterns. 2. Patchwork—Patterns. 3. Borders, Ornamental (Decorative arts). I. Title.
     TT835 .M27299 2002
     746.46'041—dc21   2002007825

MISSION STATEMENT

We are dedicated to providing quality products and service by working together to inspire creativity and to enrich the lives we touch.

CONTENTS

INTRODUCTION

Two of the most frequently asked questions I receive from novice quilters are "How should I set these blocks?" and "What kind of border should I put on my quilt?" The blocks in question may have been handed down from a grandmother or aunt, purchased at a garage sale, or won at a quilt guild drawing. Regardless of how the blocks came to be, they pose a problem if a set wasn't envisioned as the blocks were made. This is often the stopping point on a quilt project, the obstacle that brings about another unfinished project. However, a little forethought can prevent your blocks or quilt top from landing on the UFO (unfinished object) pile.

This book provides ideas for block settings and guidelines for choosing appropriate borders. I have found these guidelines to be reliable design assets in my quiltmaking, and I hope you'll find them just as valuable.

Borders provide the finishing touch to any pieced quilt. But selecting a border that best enhances the quilt is a common problem. Perhaps after the top is pieced, the quilter feels that it's finished. It's all too easy to add a plain border and call it good. However, a pieced or appliquéd border can turn an ordinary quilt into a spectacular quilt.

The quilts in this book are grouped by the type of border used on them. These borders range from simple straight-sewn or mitered borders to more elaborate appliqué borders. Directions are provided for eighteen finished quilts, with plenty of variations and creative options. Quilting suggestions give directions for the quilting you see in the photos. I hope these quilts will encourage you to think "beyond the blocks."

Nancy J. Martin

FABRIC SELECTION

FABRICS ARE OFTEN the starting point for my quilt designs. I am attracted to spectacular large-scale prints, toiles, and novelty fabrics of all types. These fabrics are dynamic when used to their best advantage in a quilt, but they can be wasted if the proper design is not chosen.

Theme prints or novelty prints feature a design that depicts a scene or other large-scale motif. Some fabric manufacturers are now producing novelty prints that feature paper dolls, cowboys, wildlife, cityscapes, food, children's toys, nursery rhymes, plants, and dishes. Since these designs are

generally quite large, the fabrics are best used in large pieces so that you can see the whole design. If you cut the fabric into small pieces, you lose the context of the fabric.

A simple setting that frames the design works best with a novelty print. This focuses attention on the detail of the design. These same simple settings also work for purchased batik blocks, photo-transfer blocks, printed squares sometimes known as cheater's cloth, and some appliqué blocks. Several of the quilts in this book present ideas for using these types of fabric. Once you determine a common size to cut your theme fabrics, select a setting that will accommodate that block size. Finished block sizes used for the quilts in this book made with a novelty print, batik blocks, or a special floral print are:

Block Size	Project
3"	Nautical Stars (page 45)
4"	Kristin's Stars (page 20)
	Tilt-a-Whirl (page 48)
6"	Courthouse Steps (page 38)
	Nursery Rhymes (page 62)
	Childhood Daze (page 66)
8"	Handkerchief Quilt (page 42)
	Setting Stars (page 85)

FUSSY CUTTING

*M*ANY NOVELTY *prints require special cutting to show them to their best advantage. I take the time to fussy cut these fabrics for my quilts, knowing that the results are well worth the effort, even though the remaining fabric looks like a piece of Swiss cheese when I am finished.*

To fussy cut a fabric, make an expandable window from two pieces of L-shaped cardboard. Place this window on the different design elements in the fabric, noting the size needed to accommodate each design. Look for a common size that will work for most of the designs; unfortunately, not all the motifs may be the same size. Once you determine a common size, add ¼"-wide seam allowances on all sides and cut the necessary pieces.

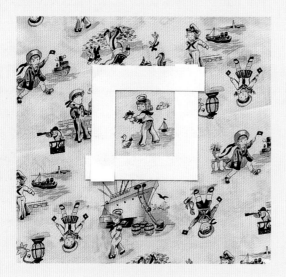

Isolate motif in window.

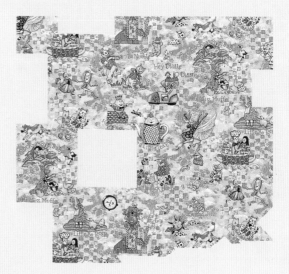

After fussy cutting, the remaining fabric looks like Swiss cheese.

With the variety of fabrics being offered today, it's hard for me to make a quilt using the tried-and-true plan of one light, one medium, and one dark fabric. I much prefer to use many different fabrics in my quilts, creating a more interesting look.

Several of the quilts in this book use a greater variety of fabrics than called for in the cutting specifications. I have listed the most economical and efficient use of fabric, but don't hesitate to add additional fabrics from your scrap basket to get a wider array of fabric. My theory has always been— "Why use two fabrics, when you can use twenty?"

If you are unsure of how to adapt standard directions to cut a multifabric quilt, try these tips:

◆ Gather appropriate amounts of fabric for each color group. If 3 yards of dark blue fabric is specified, select ½ yard each of at least six different blue prints. It sometimes helps to vary the amount of each print used within a color grouping. Some prints are too dominant and eye-catching to be used frequently; to avoid interrupting the unity of the design, use them in smaller amounts. Smaller, more restful prints that help the design flow from one area of the quilt to another can be used more often.

◆ Consult the cutting directions to see how the fabric is to be cut for the quilt. If bias squares (see page 16) are part of the cutting directions, look at the photo to see if all of the bias squares are identical or if they are used in a mix-and-match configuration. For instance, if the bias squares are to be cut from light blue and dark blue fabrics, cut two squares each from six different light blue and dark blue fabrics. When pairing the light blue and dark blue squares to cut the strips for bias squares, combine a different light blue and dark blue fabric

each time, never repeating the same fabric combination.

◆ When cutting squares and triangles, use a variety of fabrics as described at left. For example, if thirty-five total dark squares are needed, gather seven different dark fabrics and cut five squares from each dark fabric.

The fabric requirements given in this book are generous and based on yardage that is 42" wide after prewashing. If your fabric is wider than 42", there will be a little left over at the end of your strips. If your fabric is narrower than 42", you may need to cut an extra strip. Save any extra yardage or strips for future scrap quilts.

Many of the yardage amounts in this book specify fat quarters. A fat quarter is an 18" x 21" piece of fabric rather than the standard quarter yard that is cut selvage to selvage and measures 9" x 42". The fat quarter is a more convenient size to use, especially when cutting bias strips. Another common size is the fat eighth, which measures 9" x 21". Shops often offer fat quarters and fat eighths already cut and bundled. Look for them at your local quilt shop.

Border Basics

GREAT QUILTS HAVE borders that integrate with the quilt design and enhance the top. There are many possibilities, and choosing the right border is easier if you acquaint yourself with some of the options and analyze why they work. Read through "Border Basics" for an overview before planning your quilt design.

Before You Begin

Graph paper, a calculator, and a copy machine are valuable tools when I begin to plan my quilt design. I sketch one block on graph paper and then make several photocopies of it. I cut and paste these

photocopies, using both straight and diagonal sets. When I arrive at a pleasing design, I begin to look for design elements that I can repeat in the border.

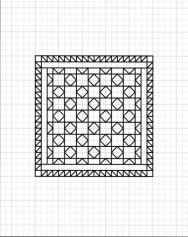

Three simple, straightforward quilt plans that are shown on page 8 illustrate this principle. The added advantage of planning your quilt this way is that you don't have to do any math calculations for these borders because the same-size design element in the border is already used in the blocks.

Sometimes it's necessary to do some mathematical calculations when designing borders. Guidelines for determining these specific calculations are included with the border-option information on the following pages.

The following border options are used in the quilts in this book. Directions for stitching borders to your quilt can be found in "Adding Borders" on pages 102–104.

Simple Borders

The simplest borders to make are unpieced borders with straight-cut corners, corner squares, or mitered corners. Unpieced borders are often cut along the crosswise grain and seamed where extra length is needed. When using large-scale prints, however, I prefer to cut borders from the lengthwise grain. This requires extra fabric, but it means you don't have a seam interrupting the design.

Keep the following guidelines in mind when considering the three simple border options that follow.

✦ Don't make the border too narrow or it may make the quilt look unfinished.

✦ Don't make the border too wide or it may overwhelm the center design.

✦ Try multiple borders in different sizes rather than one extrawide border. The additional fabrics will create more interest than just one wide border.

✦ Strive for a border that frames the quilt and focuses attention on the quilt center.

✦ Integrate borders into the quilt design—try to enhance the central design rather than distract from it.

Too Narrow

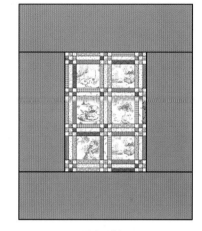

Too Wide

Multiple Borders

Borders with Straight-Cut Corners

A border with straight-cut corners is the simplest border to add and was used on several of the quilts in this book (see "Kristin's Stars" on page 20).

Borders with Corner Squares

Applying borders with corner squares provides another area where you can add an additional bit of color or creativity. It's also an economical use of fabric because you can use shorter border strips.

Borders with Mitered Corners

Mitered borders have a diagonal seam where the borders meet in the corners. See "Land of Liberty" (page 96).

This type of border is especially effective if you have a wide-stripe fabric or a large floral print. While none of the quilts in this book include a wide-stripe fabric in the border, it is important to know how to use them effectively on a quilt.

Wide-stripe fabrics, often referred to as border stripes, make wonderful borders but are among the most challenging fabrics to use. If the fabric is printed with at least four repeats across the width of fabric, it can be very economical to use. If it doesn't have four repeats across the width, you'll have to purchase twice as much yardage to use this fabric as a border.

The challenge in using border stripes is to get the stripes to miter gracefully at the corners and to have the same portion of the print do this on all four corners. To achieve this, I work from the outside in when designing my quilt. In other words, I start with the border and then design the size of the blocks and the sashing width to accommodate the border.

For example, in the quilt "Amsterdam Star" shown below (from *101 Fabulous Rotary-Cut Quilts*, Martingale & Company, 1998), I cut and laid out the borders, folding a miter in each corner. When I determined where the miter should be on each corner, I then measured the inside edge of the border and added ½" for seam allowances. This measurement came to 62½". I then subtracted 49½" (each of the three blocks measures 16½"), leaving a total of 13" for the four pieces of sashing. I divided 13" by 4" (3¼") to get the width of each sashing strip and added ½" for seam allowances, so I cut my sashing pieces 3¾" wide.

AMSTERDAM STAR

PATCHWORK BORDERS

Patchwork borders are made up of pieced units, which often repeat shapes found in the blocks. The pieced unit within the border is often called a repeat. This repeat can be simple, as in the plain squares in "Handkerchief Quilt" (page 42), or more complex, as in the delectable mountains border in "Tilt-a-Whirl" (page 48). They can even be pic-torial, as in "Cabin in the Trees" (page 70), where small trees surround the center blocks.

For a patchwork border to fit, the finished size of the quilt top must be equally divisible by the size of the border repeat. For example, if you want to repeat a 2" unit, the finished size of the quilt top must divide equally by 2. A 4" repeat will work only on a quilt top whose finished size can be equally divided by 4.

If your quilt top is not evenly divisible by the size of the border unit, you can add a spacer strip, also known as a coping strip, to bring the measurement of the quilt top up to an evenly divisible size. In addition to the coping strip, sometimes you may need to make the units slightly smaller or larger than what you used in the blocks. For example, in "Blossom Baskets" (page 57), I cut 2½" bias squares for the blocks and 2⅜" bias squares for the border.

SAWTOOTH BORDERS

If you use the same-size bias squares that are used in the quilt blocks, sawtooth borders are among the easiest borders to do.

Bias Square

Sawtooth units are so versatile in a border that there are many arrangement options to choose from. The most pleasing of these borders have an even number of units in both the lengthwise and crosswise borders so that the units change direction in the middle of the border, and all four corners are the same.

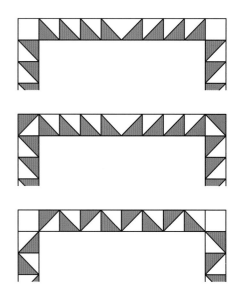

Sometimes the length and width of the quilt don't have a common divisor, so the same width of strip cannot be used for both the lengthwise and crosswise coping strips. To make the corners symmetrical, you need to use measurements divisible by the same number. In this case, I don't hesitate to use slightly different widths for the lengthwise and crosswise coping strips. This was true in "Dolly Madison's Amish Star" (page 52). In this quilt, I cut the side coping strips 3⅞" wide and the top and bottom coping strips 3½" wide.

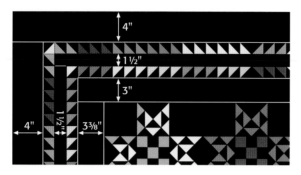

Measurements are finished sizes.

The challenge of using a sawtooth border comes when there are an uneven number of bias-square units in the border. Because you can't turn half of them in the opposite direction, there will be opposite matching corners; some very effective borders can be designed in this way.

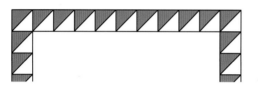

You can also use the concept of a sawtooth border to make pieced borders with bias rectangles, as shown in "54-40 or Fight" (page 77).

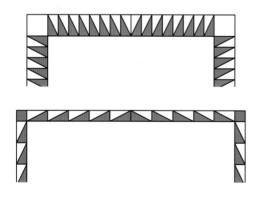

Dogtooth Borders

A dogtooth border differs from a sawtooth border in the type of triangles used. The sawtooth border,

a bias-square unit, uses half-square triangles; the dogtooth border uses quarter-square triangles.

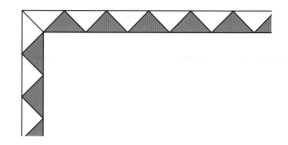

I like to frame quilts with dogtooth borders. Using a darker fabric on the outer edge of the dogtooth creates a wonderful frame for the quilt (see "Childhood Daze" on page 66). I also like to use this type of border on quilts with a mitered corner on the inner or outer borders.

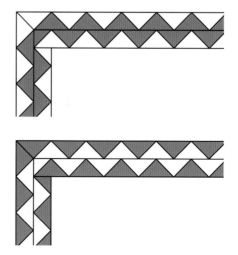

Dogtooth border with mitered inner borders.

Offsetting two rows of dogtooth borders creates a zigzag border.

Borders from Leftover Strips

Several of the borders in this book utilize the short pieces of fabric strips left over from piecing the quilt top. These can be very effective as well as economical on any Log Cabin or Courthouse Steps quilt (see "Log Cabin Barn Raising" on page 34).

Another way to utilize leftover strips is to make paper-pieced blocks for the border. Straight strips such as those shown on "Sunshine and Shadow" (page 29), string strips, or even a Crazy-patch technique can be used. Start with a foundation cut from paper and then fill in the blocks, beginning at the center of each foundation paper.

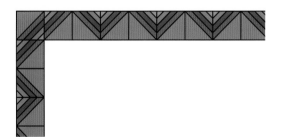

Checkerboard Borders

Checkerboard borders are a great way to enliven a quilt. They work well as middle borders and can easily be combined with a wide outer border or another pieced border, as shown in "Dick and Jane" (page 38).

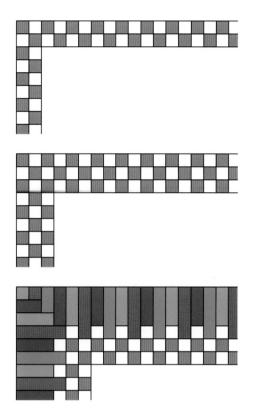

I also like to combine a smaller checkerboard border with another checkerboard border in a larger size.

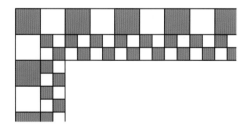

Extended-Design Borders

You can often create a spectacular design by extending the blocks into the border. You can use this technique to highlight a particular design element or to simply showcase the blocks. In "Wagon

Tracks" (page 81 and below), the triangles are emphasized as they break into the border. In "Setting Stars" (page 85 and below), the extension of the star points into the border, along with the darker fabric used in the half blocks, complete the design and focus attention on the embroidered squares. Often, just a change of fabric or color in the design elements can create an effective border.

APPLIQUÉ BORDERS

Borders that utilize appliqué can be pleasing and graceful. If the design of the quilt is angular, such as in "Hearts and Flowers" (page 91), the curved lines of the border help to soften the angular design. The appliqué border used in "Christmas Tree Farm," shown below (from *Patchwork Picnic*, Martingale & Company, 2001), is another example of how curved lines can soften an angular design.

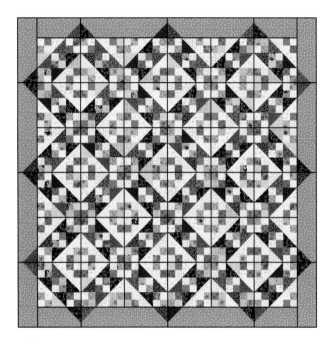

WAGON TRACKS

CHRISTMAS TREE FARM

Often the appliqué on borders can be done on individual border pieces before adding them to the quilt, making the project more portable. Additional appliqué pieces, such as the corner stars on "Land of Liberty" (page 96), can be stitched after the borders are added to the quilt top.

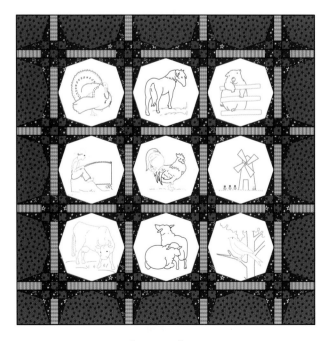

SETTING STARS

TIMESAVING TECHNIQUES

RATHER THAN PROVIDING an overview of the basics of quiltmaking, I would like to share the directions for those techniques that are specific to the projects in this book and that might not be found in your general quiltmaking books. These are timesaving techniques that have proved invaluable in my quiltmaking.

SPEED PIECING LOG CABIN BLOCKS

Sewing pieces together and then cutting them apart is an easy and quick way to make Log Cabin blocks.

1. Place the center squares on top of a strip for log 1, right sides together. Position them as close as possible without overlapping the edges. Stitch. Cut between the squares, trimming any excess fabric between the units. Press the seam away from the center square as indicated by the pressing arrow. Pressing arrows will be shown in construction diagrams throughout this book.

2. With log 1 closest to you, place the center units on top of a strip for log 2, as close as possible without overlapping the edges. Stitch. Cut between the units, trimming any excess fabric between the units. Press the seam away from the center square.

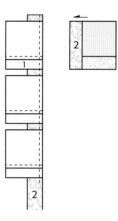

3. With log 2 closest to you, place the just-completed units on top of a strip for log 3. Stitch, trim, and press as above.

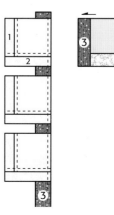

4. Continue adding strips for each log clockwise, in numerical order, to complete the Log Cabin blocks.

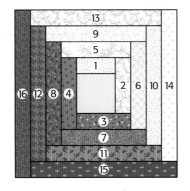

Remember, when sewing units to strips, always place the last strip you added closest to you and press the seams away from the center square.

SPEED PIECING COURTHOUSE STEPS BLOCKS

Courthouse Steps blocks are made in a similar manner to Log Cabin blocks. The rounds are added in numerical order, but they are sewn to opposite sides of the block in each round instead of in a clockwise fashion. Follow the placement diagram for the block you are making to make sure you are placing the logs correctly.

BIAS SQUARES

Many traditional quilt patterns contain squares made from two contrasting half-square triangles. The short sides of the triangles are on the straight grain of the fabric, while the long sides are on the bias. These are called bias squares. Using a bias strip-piecing method, you can easily sew and cut bias squares. This technique is especially useful for small bias squares, where pressing after stitching usually distorts the shape (and sometimes burns fingers). The following directions describe an easy way to cut bias squares from two 8" squares. The size of the squares from which to cut bias squares will vary from pattern to pattern, but the technique is the same. To use this method, you'll need the Bias Square® ruler. The Bias Square ruler is available at many quilt shops and through Martingale & Company.

NOTE: *All directions in this book give the cut size for bias squares; the finished size after stitching will be ½" smaller.*

1. Layer two 8" squares of fabric, right sides facing up, and cut in half diagonally.

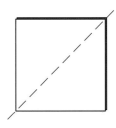

2. Cut into strips, measuring from the previous diagonal cut. Strip-width measurements are included in the quilt directions.

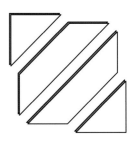

3. Arrange and stitch the pieces together, using ¼"-wide seam allowances. Be sure to align the strips so the lower edge and one adjacent edge form straight lines. Press the seams toward the darker fabric.

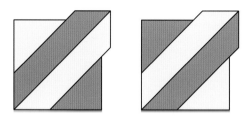

4. Begin cutting at the lower left corner. Align the 45° mark of the Bias Square ruler on the seam line. Each bias square will require 4 cuts. The first and second cuts are along the side and top edges. They remove the bias square from the rest of the fabric. Make these cuts ¼" larger than the correct size, as shown in the series of illustrations below.

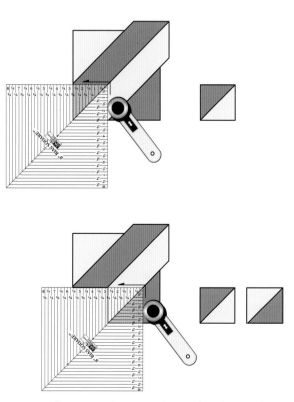

Align 45° mark on seam line and cut first 2 sides.

5. The third and fourth cuts are made along the remaining two sides. They align the diagonal and trim the bias square to the correct size. To make the cuts, turn the segment and place the Bias Square ruler on the opposite 2 sides, aligning the required measurements on both sides of the cutting guide and the 45° mark on the seam. Cut the remaining 2 sides of the bias square.

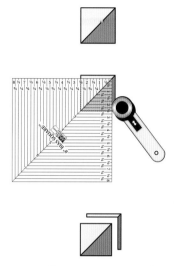

Turn cut segments and cut opposite 2 sides.

6. Continue cutting bias squares from each unit in this manner, working from left to right and from bottom to top, until you have cut bias squares from all usable fabric.

BIAS RECTANGLES

Bias rectangles are used to make the pieced units in "54-40 or Fight" (page 77). These units are made in a similar manner to bias squares, except instead of cutting a square from the pieced fabric, you cut a rectangle. You will need the BiRangle™ ruler to cut bias rectangles.

1. Layer two 12" x 42" rectangles, right sides facing up. Fold the fabrics in half and place the fold on the left. Place the BiRangle ruler on the upper edge of the fabrics so that the diagonal line points from the upper edge of the fabrics to the lower right-hand corner. (The angle line of the ruler will be about 5¾" from the selvage edge.)

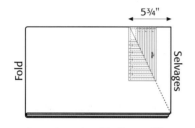

Place BiRangle with diagonal line pointing toward lower right-hand corner.

2. Lay a long ruler on the diagonal line of the BiRangle. This creates an angle across the fabric.

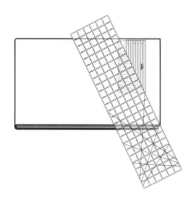

3. Holding the long ruler in place, slide the BiRangle out of the way. Cut along the right-hand edge of the ruler on the diagonal.

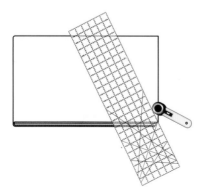

4. Cut 6 sets of strips, each 2½" wide, parallel to this first angled cut. Don't move the strips yet. Without disturbing the strips, remove the large leftover end pieces and set them aside. Save these for another project.

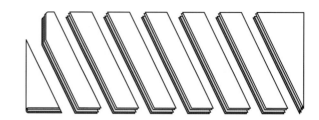

5. Because the fabrics were folded, some strips will have right sides facing up and some will have right sides facing down. Sort the strips into 2 sets, placing the up-facing ones on the right and the down-facing ones on the left. Arrange the 12 strips on the right, without turning any over, into a unit of strips, alternating the fabrics. With right sides together, sew the strips, offsetting the tops ¼" so that they form an even-angled line across the top of the unit.

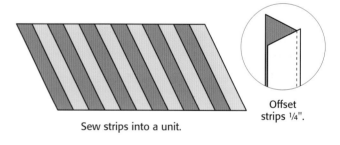

Sew strips into a unit.

Offset strips ¼".

6. Press the seams open. Don't worry if one edge of the unit is a bit ragged.

7. Arrange, sew, and press the strips on the left into a unit. The strips will slope in the opposite direction from the first set.

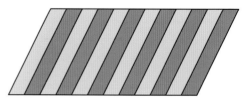

Left set slopes in opposite direction.

8. Continue to sew units of 12 strips as needed for your quilt, keeping the up-facing sets separated from the down-facing sets.

9. For units that slant to the left, begin cutting at the lower right-hand corner. Align the diagonal line of the BiRangle on the seam line. Each rectangle will require 4 cuts. The first and second cuts are along the side and top edges. They remove the rectangle from the rest of the fabric. Make these cuts ¼" larger than the correct size.

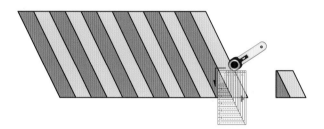

10. The third and fourth cuts are made along the remaining 2 sides and the rectangle is trimmed to the correct size. To make the cuts, turn the segment and place the BiRangle on the opposite 2 sides, aligning the required measurements on both sides of the cutting guide and the diagonal line of the ruler on the seam. Cut the remaining 2 sides of the bias rectangle.

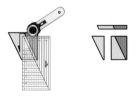

11. Continue cutting bias rectangles from each unit in this manner, working from right to left and from bottom to top, until you have cut bias rectangles from all usable fabric.

12. For units that slant to the right, begin cutting at the lower left-hand corner. Turn the BiRangle over to cut these rectangles.

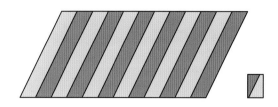

Bias-Strip Appliqué

The following steps describe the bias-strip appliqué process.

1. Cut bias strips according to the measurements indicated in the quilt directions.

2. Fold each bias strip in half, wrong sides together, and stitch ⅛" from the edges. Press the tube so that the seam falls in the middle on the back side.

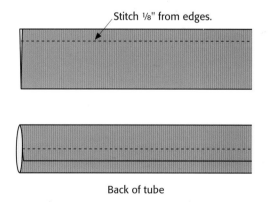

Stitch ⅛" from edges.

Back of tube

3. Place the bias tube on the background fabric, forming the desired shape. Pin and stitch in place.

KRISTIN'S STARS

KRISTIN'S STARS BY KRISTIN ADAMS, 2000, REDMOND, WASHINGTON, 65" x 65".
QUILTED BY ALVINA NELSON, SALINA, KANSAS.

A DIAGONAL SET *is an effective way to showcase a delightful print in the unpieced setting squares. In this case, Provençal fabrics are used in the setting squares and Star blocks, and then the blocks are set together with a light print in the triangular background pieces. A simple multiple border enhances the spectacular center.*

MATERIALS

Yardage is based on 42"-wide fabric.

- 9 fat quarters of assorted dark prints for star tips
- 2 yds. brick red print for outer border
- 1¾ yds. light print for blocks and setting triangles
- 6 fat eighths of assorted medium prints for large triangles
- ¾ yd. large-scale floral print for setting squares and star centers
- ½ yd. green print for inner border
- 1 fat eighth of small yellow print for blocks
- 4 yds. fabric for backing
- ⅝ yd. fabric for bias binding
- 69" x 69" piece of batting

CUTTING

All measurements include ¼"-wide seam allowances.

From the light print, cut:
- 2 squares, 18¼" x 18¼"; cut twice diagonally to yield 8 side setting triangles

- 2 squares, 9⅜" x 9⅜"; cut once diagonally to yield 4 corner triangles
- 18 squares, 5¼" x 5¼"; cut twice diagonally to yield 72 triangles
- 18 squares, 3¼" x 3¼"; cut twice diagonally to yield 72 triangles
- 72 squares, 2½" x 2½"

From the 6 assorted medium prints, cut a total of:
- 9 squares, 5¼" x 5¼"; cut twice diagonally to yield 36 triangles

From the 9 assorted dark prints, cut a total of:
- 72 squares, 2⅞" x 2⅞"; cut once diagonally to yield 144 triangles

From the small yellow print, cut:
- 36 squares, 1¹⁵⁄₁₆" x 1¹⁵⁄₁₆" (halfway between the 1⅞" and 2" marks on your ruler)

From the large-scale floral print, cut:
- 4 squares, 12½" x 12½"
- 9 squares, 4½" x 4½"

From the green print, cut:
- 6 strips, 2" x 42"

From the lengthwise grain of the brick red print, cut:
- 4 strips, 5¾" x 65"

MAKING THE BLOCKS

1. Join 2 light 5¼" triangles, 1 medium 5¼" triangle, and 2 dark 2⅞" triangles to make an outer side unit. Make 4 matching units for each block.

Make 4 matching units
for each block (36 total).

ON A SLANT

For a diagonally set quilt, the straight of grain for the side triangles should fall along the outside edge, while the straight of grain for the corner triangles should fall along both outside edges to prevent sagging or ruffled edges. To assure that the straight of grain will be placed correctly, cut half-square and quarter-square triangles as specified in the directions.

When you set blocks diagonally, it is helpful to know the diagonal measurement of the block so that you can compute the quilt size. To determine the diagonal measurement, multiply the length of one side of the block by 1.414 or use the chart.

⬦ Diagonal Measurement		
4" block	=	5⅝"
5" block	=	7⅛"
6" block	=	8½"
7" block	=	9⅞"
8" block	=	11¼"
9" block	=	12¾"
10" block	=	14⅛"
12" block	=	17"
14" block	=	19⅞"
16" block	=	22⅝"
18" block	=	25½"
20" block	=	28¼"
24" block	=	34"

2. Join 2 light 3¼" triangles, 1 yellow 1¹⁵⁄₁₆" square, and 2 dark 2⅞" triangles to make an inner side unit. Make 4 matching units for each block.

Make 4 matching units
for each block (36 total).

3. Join 4 matching outer side units, 4 matching inner side units, 1 floral 4½" square, and 8 light 2½" squares to make a block.

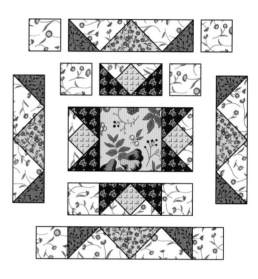

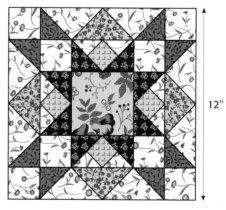

12"

Make 9.

ASSEMBLING THE QUILT

Arrange and sew the blocks, 12½" floral squares, and 18¼" side setting triangles in diagonal rows. Join the rows. Add a 9⅜" triangle to each corner.

ADDING THE BORDERS

1. Referring to "Borders with Straight-Cut Corners" on page 102 and joining the strips as needed, measure and trim the 2"-wide green inner borders and sew them to the quilt top.

2. Measure and trim the 5¾"-wide red outer borders and sew them to the quilt top as for the inner border.

FINISHING THE QUILT

1. Layer the quilt top with batting and backing; baste and quilt as desired. *Quilting suggestion:* Quilt each star in the ditch. Quilt a medallion pattern in the center of each floral square, and partial medallions in the setting triangles. Quilt an elongated crescent pattern in the inner border, and a snowflake and crosshatch pattern in the outer border.

2. Referring to "Bias Binding" on page 107, cut and piece approximately 270" of bias binding and bind the edges of the quilt.

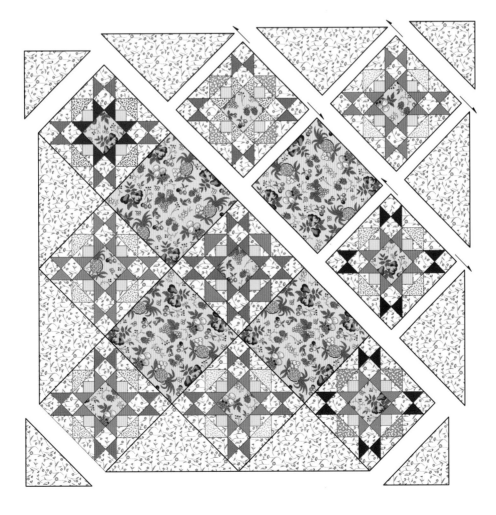

CREATIVE CURVES BY NANCY J. MARTIN, 2001, WOODINVILLE, WASHINGTON, 50½" x 50½".
QUILTED BY EDNA BORNTREGER, LA RUE, OHIO.

*C*URVED SASHING IS *great when used with angular blocks, especially Star blocks. Alternating the direction of the inner and outer curves creates an undulating effect along the edges. Such unusual sashing calls for a plain, wide border to showcase the curves and keep the attention on the center of the quilt.*

MATERIALS

Yardage is based on 42"-wide fabric.

- 1½ yds. light taupe print for sashing and border
- 6 fat quarters of assorted black prints for blocks and sashing
- 6 fat quarters of assorted taupe prints for blocks and sashing
- 6 fat eighths of assorted light prints for blocks
- 3 yds. fabric for backing
- ½ yd. fabric for bias binding
- 54" x 54" piece of batting

CUTTING

All measurements include ¼"-wide seam allowances.

From the 6 assorted black prints, cut a total of:
- 36 squares, 2" x 2"
- 9 squares, 4¼" x 4¼"; cut twice diagonally to yield 36 triangles
- 4 pieces, 1½" x 2½"
- 4 pieces, 1½" x 3½"
- 12 of template 1 (page 28)
- 12 of template 2 (page 28)

From the 6 assorted light prints, cut a total of:
- 36 squares, 2" x 2"
- 36 pieces, 2" x 3½"
- 9 squares, 4¼" x 4¼"; cut twice diagonally to yield 36 triangles

From the 6 assorted taupe prints, cut a total of:
- 27 squares, 4¼" x 4¼"; cut twice diagonally to yield 108 triangles
- 4 squares, 1½" x 1½"
- 4 pieces, 1½" x 2½"
- 6 of template 1 (page 28)
- 6 of template 2 (page 28)

From the lengthwise grain of the light taupe print, cut:
- 4 strips, 6" x 50½"
- 12 squares, 3½" x 3½"
- 4 squares, 1½" x 1½"
- 6 of template 1 (page 28)
- 6 of template 2 (page 28)

Making the Blocks

1. Join 1 black 2" square, 1 light 2" square, and 1 matching light 2" x 3½" piece to make a corner unit. Make 4 matching units for each block.

Make 4 matching units
for each block (36 total).

2. Join 1 light triangle, 1 black triangle, and 2 matching taupe triangles to make a star tip. Make 4 matching units for each block.

Make 4 matching units
for each block (36 total).

3. Join 4 taupe triangles, 2 each of 2 different prints, to make a center unit.

Make 9.

4. Join 4 matching corner units, 4 matching star tips, and 1 center unit to make a block.

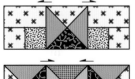

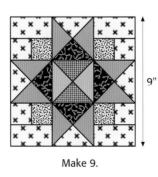

Make 9.

Assembling the Quilt

1. Join pieces cut with templates 1 and 2, right sides together, to make the following sashing units. With piece 2 on top, pin the ends and the corners. Add pins as necessary to ease the curves together. Stitch along the curved edge.

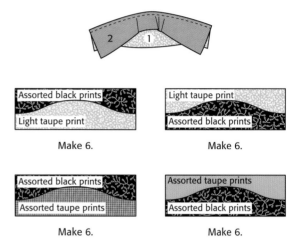

Assorted black prints / Light taupe print — Make 6.

Light taupe print / Assorted black prints — Make 6.

Assorted black prints / Assorted taupe prints — Make 6.

Assorted taupe prints / Assorted black prints — Make 6.

2. Join the 1½"-wide black, assorted taupe, and light taupe pieces as shown to make each of 4 pieced sashing squares.

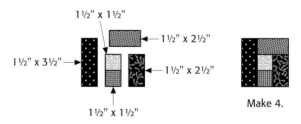

1½" x 1½"
1½" x 2½"
1½" x 3½"
1½" x 2½"
1½" x 1½"
Make 4.

3. Arrange and sew the blocks, pieced sashing units, 3½" light taupe sashing squares, and pieced sashing squares into rows as shown, referring to the color photo on page 24 for color placement. Join the rows.

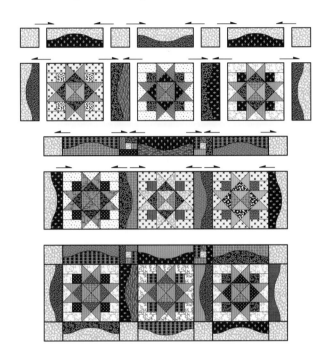

ADDING THE BORDER

Referring to "Borders with Straight-Cut Corners" on page 102, measure and trim the 6"-wide taupe borders and sew them to the quilt top.

FINISHING THE QUILT

1. Layer the quilt top with batting and backing; baste and quilt as desired. *Quilting suggestion:* Quilt the blocks and pieced sashing squares in the ditch. Outline-quilt the curved sashing strips and large sashing squares, and quilt a cable pattern in the border.

2. Referring to "Bias Binding" on page 107, cut and piece approximately 215" of bias binding and bind the edges of the quilt.

OTHER OPTION

"Anchors Aweigh," below, illustrates another design option. Narrow sashing strips were used between the blocks, and the curved sashing pieces along the outer edges of the blocks create a curved border effect.

ANCHORS AWEIGH
BY NANCY J. MARTIN, 2001,
WOODINVILLE, WASHINGTON, 35½" x 35½".

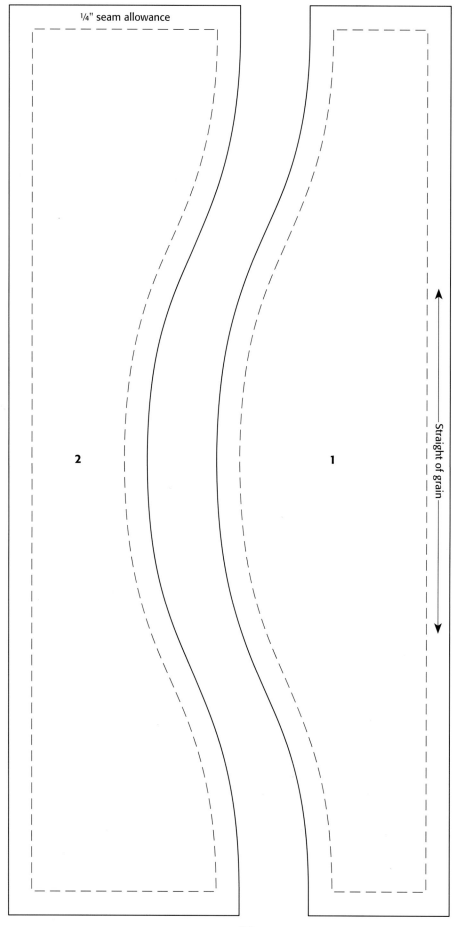

¼" seam allowance

2

1

Straight of grain

SUNSHINE AND SHADOW

SUNSHINE AND SHADOW BY NANCY J. MARTIN AND CLEO NOLLETTE, 2000, WOODINVILLE, WASHINGTON, 76½" x 76½". QUILTED BY ANNA STUTZMAN, KENTON, OHIO.

Tʜɪꜱ ʟᴏɢ ᴄᴀʙɪɴ *quilt, set in the Sunshine and Shadow pattern, is framed by a delight-fully easy paper-pieced border that makes use of the leftover strips.*

Mᴀᴛᴇʀɪᴀʟꜱ

Yardage is based on 42"-wide fabric.

- ½ yd. *each* of 10 assorted medium blue prints for blocks and border
- ½ yd. *each* of 8 assorted light prints for blocks and border
- ⅜ yd. yellow print for block centers
- 5 yds. fabric for backing
- ⅝ yd. fabric for bias binding
- 80" x 80" piece of batting
- 28 sheets of 8½" x 11" foundation paper

Cᴜᴛᴛɪɴɢ

All measurements include ¼"-wide seam allowances.

From the yellow print, cut:
- 36 squares, 2½" x 2½"

From *each* of the 8 light prints, cut:
- 9 strips, 1½" x 42" (72 total)

From *each* of the 10 medium blue prints, cut:
- 10 strips, 1½" x 42" (100 total)

Mᴀᴋɪɴɢ ᴛʜᴇ Bʟᴏᴄᴋꜱ

Referring to "Speed Piecing Log Cabin Blocks" on page 15 and following the chart below for fabric placement, make 36 Log Cabin blocks. Join the pieces to the yellow center in numerical order. Select the fabrics randomly to create a scrappy look.

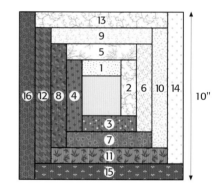

Piecing Diagram

Round 1	Light	Pieces 1, 2
	Medium blue	Pieces 3, 4
Round 2	Light	Pieces 5, 6
	Medium blue	Pieces 7, 8
Round 3	Light	Pieces 9, 10
	Medium blue	Pieces 11, 12
Round 4	Light	Pieces 13, 14
	Medium blue	Pieces 15, 16

Assembling the Quilt

Arrange and sew the blocks into 6 rows of 6 blocks each. Rotate the blocks as needed to create the Sunshine and Shadow setting. Join the rows.

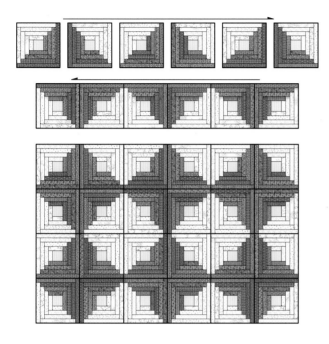

Adding the Border

1. Trim 24 sheets of foundation paper to 8½" x 10½", and 4 sheets to 8½" x 8½".

2. Draw a diagonal line at a 45° angle on 12 of the 8½" x 10½" foundation papers, beginning in the upper left corner. Draw a diagonal line on the remaining 8½" x 10½" foundation papers, beginning in the upper right corner. The larger section of the paper will be covered by medium blue strips, and the smaller section by light strips.

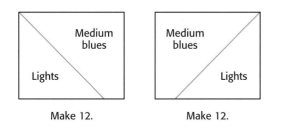

Make 12.   Make 12.

3. Place a medium blue strip, right side up, so that the left edge of the strip is ¼" beyond the drawn line. Baste in place.

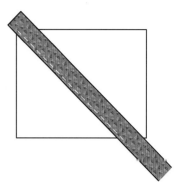

4. Place another medium blue strip on the first medium blue strip, right sides together, so that the long edges on the right-hand sides are aligned. Stitch along this edge with a ¼" seam.

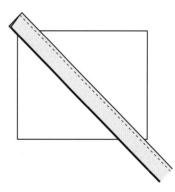

5. Open and press the second medium blue strip. Trim both strips along the edge of the paper.

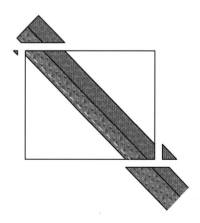

6. Continue adding medium blue strips until the corner of the paper is covered. Use short strips left over from the block piecing for the corners.

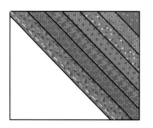

7. Starting in the center and working toward the corner, add light strips to the opposite corner of the foundation paper in the same manner as the medium blue strips. Make 24 border blocks. Don't remove the paper yet.

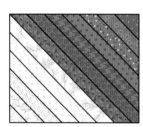

Make 12.

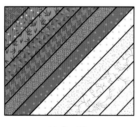

Make 12.

8. For the corner blocks, draw a diagonal line from corner to corner on each 8½" square of foundation paper.

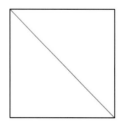

9. Using the same procedure described in steps 3–7, cover one-half of the foundation paper with medium blue strips and the other half with light strips. Don't remove the paper yet.

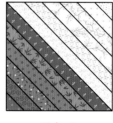

Make 4.

10. Sew 6 border blocks together as shown to make each of 4 borders.

Make 4.

11. With the paper still in place, stitch 2 borders to opposite sides of the quilt top, matching the seam lines.

12. Add a corner block to each end of the 2 remaining borders and add these to the top and bottom of the quilt.

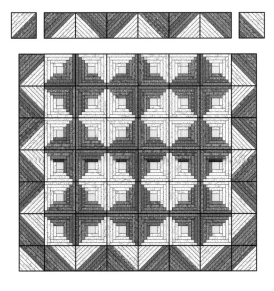

13. Tug gently on the opposite corners of each square to release the paper from the seam. Remove the paper from the border blocks.

FINISHING THE QUILT

1. Layer the quilt top with batting and backing; baste and quilt as desired. *Quilting suggestion:* Quilt the strips of the Log Cabin blocks down the center. Quilt the border blocks in the ditch.

2. Referring to "Bias Binding" on page 107, cut and piece approximately 330" of bias binding and bind the edges of the quilt.

RIP OFF

The border construction for this project differs from standard paper piecing in that the foundation paper is used as a stabilizer. All of the strips are sewn together on top of the paper using ¼" seams.

The paper remains behind the border until the final step. The following tips prove helpful in removing the paper.

1. Use a large needle (size 90/14).

2. Set your machine to a short stitch (18 to 20 stitches per inch).

3. Gently tug at the opposite corners of each border square to loosen paper.

4. Remove any stubborn bits of remaining paper with tweezers.

LOG CABIN BARN RAISING

LOG CABIN BARN RAISING BY NANCY J. MARTIN, 2000, WOODINVILLE, WASHINGTON, 75" x 75".
QUILTED BY ALVINA NELSON, SALINA, KANSAS.

The BARN RAISING *setting can be used for many different blocks, but it is most commonly used with Log Cabin blocks. This particular quilt is unique in several ways. The red centers are larger than usual, the red is repeated in the second round of the Log Cabin blocks, and the light side of the blocks is pieced entirely with muslin strips. The diagonal strip-pieced border is a good way to use all of those small leftover pieces.*

MATERIALS

Yardage is based on 42"-wide fabric.

- 3¼ yds. muslin for blocks, inner border, and pieced border
- ¼ yd. *each* of 11 assorted dark prints (tan, brown, and black) for blocks and pieced border
- 1½ yds. red print for blocks and pieced border
- ½ yd. white shirting print for blocks
- 4¾ yds. fabric for backing
- ⅝ yd. fabric for bias binding
- 79" x 79" piece of batting

CUTTING

All measurements include ¼"-wide seam allowances.

From the red print, cut:
- 3 strips, 3" x 42"; crosscut strips into 36 squares, 3" x 3"
- 22 strips, 1½" x 42"

From the muslin, cut:
- 60 strips, 1½" x 42"
- 7 strips, 2½" x 42"

From the white shirting print, cut:
- 9 strips, 1½" x 42"

From *each* of the 11 assorted dark prints, cut:
- 5 strips, 1½" x 42" (55 total)

MAKING THE BLOCKS

Referring to "Speed Piecing Log Cabin blocks" on page 15 and following the chart below for fabric placement, make 36 Log Cabin blocks. Join the pieces to the red center in numerical order. Select dark prints randomly for rounds 11, 12, 15, and 16 to create a scrappy look.

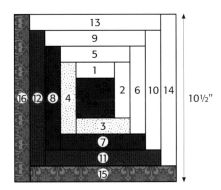

Piecing Diagram

Round 1	Muslin	Pieces 1, 2
	Shirting	Pieces 3, 4
Round 2	Muslin	Pieces 5, 6
	Red	Pieces 7, 8
Round 3	Muslin	Pieces 9, 10
	Dark	Pieces 11, 12
Round 4	Muslin	Pieces 13, 14
	Dark	Pieces 15, 16

ASSEMBLING THE QUILT

Arrange and sew the blocks into 6 rows of 6 blocks each. Rotate the blocks as needed to form the Barn Raising setting. Join the rows.

ADDING THE BORDERS

1. Referring to "Borders with Straight-Cut Corners" on page 102 and joining strips as needed, measure and trim the 2½"-wide muslin inner borders and sew them to the quilt top.

2. From the leftover red strips, cut 72 pieces, 1½" x 5". It may be necessary to cut more strips from the red print.

3. From the leftover dark strips, cut 144 pieces, 1½" x 5". It may be necessary to cut more strips from remaining fabric.

4. From the remaining muslin strips, cut 192 pieces, 1½" x 2¾".

5. Sew the 1½" x 2¾" muslin pieces to the 1½" x 5" red and dark pieces. There will be some red and dark strips left over.

Make 192.

6. Join 48 units as shown to make each of 4 pieced borders, alternating 2 dark units, a red unit, 2 dark units, a red unit, and so on. Offset the muslin pieces by 1" as you stitch the units together.

Make 4.

7. Sew additional strips to the left end of each border, creating enough length to miter the corners.

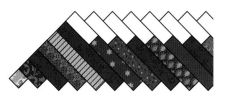

8. Working from the muslin side of the border first, place the edge of a long ruler along the intersections of the units. Trim off the muslin points. Turn the border around and trim the other edge of the border 4¼" from the just-trimmed edge.

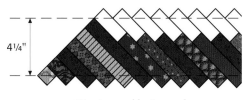

4¼"

Trim top and bottom edges.

GETTING IT STRAIGHT

It is impossible to rotary cut strips for Log Cabin blocks exactly on the straight grain of fabric since many fabrics are printed off grain. In rotary cutting, straight, even cuts are made as close to the grain as possible. A slight variation from the grain will not affect the result of your project. If fabric is badly off grain, pull diagonally to straighten, as shown.

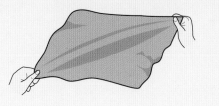

9. Referring to "Borders with Mitered Corners" on page 104, sew the pieced borders to the quilt and miter the corners.

FINISHING THE QUILT

1. Layer the quilt top with batting and backing; baste and quilt as desired. *Quilting suggestion:* Quilt the center square and dark side of the Log Cabin blocks in the ditch. Quilt a graceful rope pattern across the muslin strips. Quilt a small crescent and diamond pattern in the narrow border. Quilt the diagonal pieced border in the ditch.

2. Referring to "Bias Binding" on page 107, cut and piece approximately 310" of bias binding and bind the edges of the quilt.

COURTHOUSE STEPS

QUILTS WITH BORDERS FROM LEFTOVER STRIPS

DICK AND JANE BY NANCY J. MARTIN, 2000, WOODINVILLE, WASHINGTON, 48½" x 60½".
QUILTED BY MATTIE AND MARY MAST, FREDERICKSBURG, OHIO.

THIS CHARMING *novelty print, featuring childhood favorites Dick and Jane, is framed in a Courthouse Steps block. Leftover strips are then combined with a red-and-white checkerboard pattern to create a lively border.*

MATERIALS

Yardage is based on 42"-wide fabric.

- ¼ yd. *each* of 6 assorted tan prints for blocks and border
- ¼ yd. *each* of 6 assorted green prints for blocks and border
- ¼ yd. *each* of 6 assorted red prints for blocks and borders
- ¼ yd. *each* of 6 assorted blue prints for blocks and border
- 1 yd. novelty print for blocks*
- ½ yd. light print for border
- 3 yds. fabric for backing
- ½ yd. fabric for bias binding
- 52" x 64" piece of batting

Additional yardage may be needed to fussy cut the squares (see page 6).

CUTTING

All measurements include ¼"-wide seam allowances.

From the novelty print, fussy cut:
- 13 squares, 6½" x 6½"

From *each* of the 6 assorted tan prints, cut:
- 2 strips, 1½" x 42" (12 total)

From *each* of the 6 assorted green prints, cut:
- 2 strips, 1½" x 42" (12 total)

From *each* of the 6 assorted red prints, cut:
- 4 strips, 1½" x 42" (24 total)

From *each* of the 6 assorted blue prints, cut:
- 3 strips, 1½" x 42" (18 total)

From the light print, cut:
- 10 strips, 1½" x 42"; crosscut 3 of the strips into 84 squares, 1½" x 1½"

MAKING THE BLOCKS

Referring to "Speed Piecing Courthouse Steps Blocks" on page 16, stitch 12 Courthouse Steps blocks. Selecting fabrics randomly to create a scrappy look, begin with tan and green strips on opposite sides of the novelty-print center square. Use red strips on the top and blue strips on the bottom.

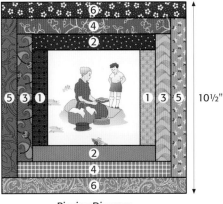

Piecing Diagram

Assembling the Quilt

Arrange and sew the blocks into 4 rows of 3 blocks each. Join the rows.

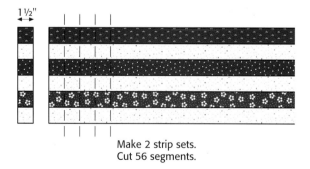

Adding the Borders

1. Join 3 red strips and 3 light strips as shown to make a strip set. Make another strip set. Cut 56 segments, each 1½" wide, from the strip sets.

1½"

Make 2 strip sets.
Cut 56 segments.

2. Join 12 red-and-light segments as shown to make a top border. Repeat for the bottom border. Sew 16 red-and-light segments together as shown for each side border.

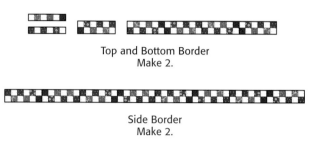

Top and Bottom Border
Make 2.

Side Border
Make 2.

3. For the "up and down" outer borders, use leftover strips to cut 21 pieces, 1½" x 3½", from each color (84 total) and 21 pieces, 1½" x 4½", from each color (84 total).

4. Sew the light squares to one end of the 1½" x 3½" colored pieces.

5. Starting with a pieced unit, join 18 pieced units and 18 of the 4½"-long pieces to make each of the top and bottom borders. Join 24 pieced units and 24 of the 4½"-long pieces to make each side border.

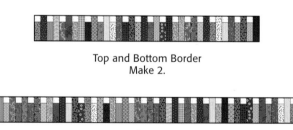

Top and Bottom Border
Make 2.

Side Border
Make 2.

6. Join the "up and down" borders and the checkerboard borders for the top and bottom edges, and stitch them to the quilt top.

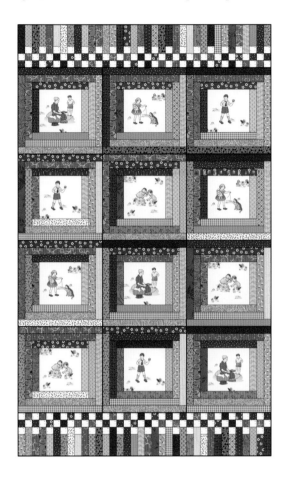

7. From leftover strips, cut and join 1½" red and light squares as shown to make a nine-patch unit.

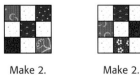

Make 2.   Make 2.

8. Sew blue strips in numerical order to 2 sides of the nine-patch units for each corner unit.

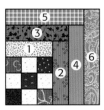
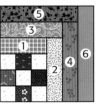

Make 2.   Make 2.

9. Sew a corner unit to each end of the 2 remaining borders, orienting the nine-patch units as shown to continue the checkerboard pattern. Add these to the sides of the quilt.

FINISHING THE QUILT

1. Layer the quilt top with batting and backing; baste and quilt as desired. *Quilting suggestion:* Outline-quilt the motifs in the novelty print. Quilt the remainder of the blocks and the borders in the ditch.

2. Referring to "Bias Binding" on page 107, cut and piece approximately 230" of bias binding and bind the edges of the quilt.

MEGAN'S HANKIES BY NANCY J. MARTIN, 2001, WOODINVILLE, WASHINGTON, 36¼" x 46¾".
QUILTED BY WYNONA HARRINGTON, SPARTANSBURG, PENNSYLVANIA.

THIS PLAYFUL *child's quilt is made from children's handkerchiefs printed with nursery rhymes. Novelty prints or squares of printed fabric (cheater cloth) could easily be substituted. The bright bias-square border adds a punch of color, as does the bright yellow border.*

MATERIALS

Yardage is based on 42"-wide fabric.

- ¾ yd. bright yellow print for outer border
- 6 children's handkerchiefs, approximately 9½" to 10" square, for block centers
- 6 fat eighths of assorted bright dotted prints for sashing and pieced border
- 6 fat eighths of assorted light dotted prints for sashing and pieced border
- 1½ yds. fabric for backing
- ⅜ yd. fabric for bias binding
- 40" x 50" piece of batting
- Bias Square ruler to cut bias squares

CUTTING

All measurements include ¼"-wide seam allowances.

For each handkerchief:
- Square up to measure 9¼" x 9¼"

From the 6 assorted bright dotted prints, cut a total of:
- 9 squares, 7" x 7"
- 50 squares, 2¼" x 2¼"

From the 6 assorted light dotted prints, cut a total of:
- 9 squares, 7" x 7"
- 50 squares, 2¼" x 2¼"

From the bright yellow print, cut:
- 4 strips, 5¼" x 42"

ASSEMBLING THE QUILT

1. Join 5 assorted bright and light 2¼" squares to make a sashing strip.

Make 9.

2. Join 2 handkerchiefs and 3 sashing strips to make a handkerchief row.

Make 3.

3. Join 13 assorted bright and light 2¼" squares to make a sashing row.

Make 4.

4. Join the handkerchief rows and sashing rows.

ADDING THE BORDERS

1. Pair each 7" bright square with a 7" light square, right sides up. Referring to "Bias Squares" on page 16, cut and piece 2¼"-wide strips, and then cut 66 bias squares, 2¼" x 2¼".

Cut 66.

2. Join 13 bias squares as shown to make a top and bottom pieced border. Sew these to the top and bottom edges of the quilt top.

Make 2.

3. Join 20 bias squares to make each of 2 side pieced borders. Add a 2¼" light square to the right end of each border. Join these to the quilt top.

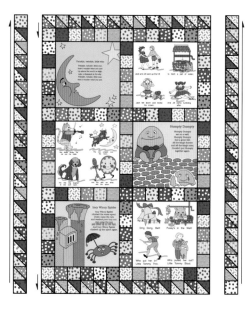

4. Referring to "Borders with Straight-Cut Corners" on page 102, measure and trim the 5¼"-wide outer borders and sew them to the quilt top.

FINISHING THE QUILT

1. Layer the quilt top with batting and backing; baste and quilt as desired. *Quilting suggestion:* Outline-quilt the motifs in the handkerchiefs and the small squares. Quilt the bias squares in the ditch. Quilt a cable pattern in the outer border.

2. Referring to "Bias Binding" on page 107, cut and piece approximately 170" of bias binding and bind the edges of the quilt.

NAUTICAL STARS

NAUTICAL *STARS* BY NANCY J. MARTIN, 2001, WOODINVILLE, WASHINGTON, 36" x 36".
QUILTED BY MRS. TOBIAS MAST, KENTON, OHIO.

THIS CHARMING *wall hanging uses an eye-catching novelty print and a patriotic color scheme. A navy star print enlivened with red-and-white stripes frames the sailor boys and girls. A calming white border surrounds both sides of the bright red sawtooth border. Notice how the bias squares change direction in the middle of each sawtooth border. This is because there are an even number of bias squares on each side of the border (see "Patchwork Borders" on page 11).*

MATERIALS

Yardage is based on 42"-wide fabric.

- 1⅜ yds. white solid for bias squares and borders
- ½ yd. novelty print for alternate blocks*
- ½ yd. red star print for bias squares
- ⅜ yd. navy blue star print for blocks
- ¼ yd. red stripe for blocks
- 1¼ yds. fabric for backing
- ⅜ yd. fabric for bias binding
- 40" x 40" piece of batting
- Bias Square ruler to cut bias squares

Additional yardage may be needed to fussy cut the squares (see page 6).

CUTTING

All measurements include ¼"-wide seam allowances.

From the navy blue star print, cut:
- 4 strips, 2⅜" x 42"; crosscut strips into 64 squares, 2⅜" x 2⅜". Cut squares once diagonally to yield 128 triangles.

From the red stripe, cut:
- 2 strips, 2⅝" x 42"; crosscut strips into 24 squares, 2⅝" x 2⅝"

From the white solid, cut:
- 4 strips, 2" x 42"
- 4 strips, 3¼" x 42"
- 9 squares, 7" x 7"
- 4 squares, 4¼" x 4¼"; cut twice diagonally to yield 16 triangles
- 12 pieces, 2" x 3½"
- 8 squares, 2" x 2"

From the novelty print, fussy cut:
- 25 squares, 3½" x 3½"

From the red star print, cut:
- 9 squares, 7" x 7"

ASSEMBLING THE QUILT

1. Sew 4 navy triangles to a red stripe square to make unit 1. Sew 2 navy triangles to a white triangle to make unit 2.

Unit 1
Make 24.

Unit 2
Make 16.

2. Arrange and sew unit 1 and unit 2, novelty print squares, 2" white squares, and 2" x 3½" white pieces into horizontal rows. Join the rows.

ADDING THE BORDERS

1. Pair a 7" white square with a 7" red star-print square, right sides up. Referring to "Bias Squares" on page 16, cut and piece 2"-wide strips, and then cut 72 bias squares, 2" x 2".

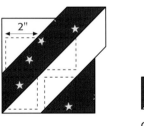

Cut 72.

2. Referring to "Borders with Straight-Cut Corners" on page 102, measure and trim the 2"-wide white inner borders and sew them to the quilt top.

3. Join 18 bias squares, 9 facing in each direction, to make each of 4 middle borders.

4. Sew 2 middle borders to opposite sides of the quilt top.

5. Add a 2" white square to each end of the 2 remaining middle borders and add these to the top and bottom edges.

6. Measure and trim the 3¼"-wide white outer borders and sew them to the quilt top as for the inner border.

FINISHING THE QUILT

1. Layer the quilt top with batting and backing; baste and quilt as desired. *Quilting suggestion:* Outline-quilt each square and triangle. Quilt a wave pattern in the inner border and a rope pattern in the outer border.

2. Referring to "Bias Binding" on page 107, cut and piece approximately 155" of bias binding and bind the edges of the quilt.

TILT-A-WHIRL

DOLPHINS BY NANCY J. MARTIN, 2000, WOODINVILLE, WASHINGTON, 24⅝" x 24⅝".
QUILTED BY WYNONA HARRINGTON, SPARTANSBURG, PENNSYLVANIA.

T HE TILT-A-WHIRL *set is the perfect setting for these purchased batik blocks. The blocks are framed by a simple inner border and an outer border made from Delectable Mountains blocks, which also use batik prints.*

MATERIALS

Yardage is based on 42"-wide fabric.

- 6 fat quarters of assorted batik prints for blocks
- ½ yd. light batik print for outer border
- ½ yd. medium batik print for outer border
- 1 fat eighth of dark batik print for inner border
- 9 batik squares, 4½" x 4½", for blocks
- ⅞ yd. fabric for backing
- ⅜ yd. fabric for bias binding
- 27" x 27" piece of batting
- Bias Square ruler to cut bias squares

CUTTING

All measurements include ¼"-wide seam allowances.

From *each* of the 6 assorted batik prints, cut:
- 6 of template 1 (36 total, page 51)

From the dark batik print, cut:
- 4 strips, 1⅞" x 21"

From the light batik print, cut:
- 4 pieces, 8" x 12"
- 4 squares, 4⅛" x 4⅛"; cut twice diagonally to yield 16 triangles
- 10 squares, 1⅞" x 1⅞"; cut once diagonally to yield 20 triangles

From the medium batik print, cut:
- 4 pieces, 8" x 12"
- 3 squares, 5½" x 5½"; cut twice diagonally to yield 12 triangles
- 2 squares, 6⅞" x 6⅞"; cut twice diagonally to yield 8 triangles
- 16 squares, 1½" x 1½"

MAKING THE BLOCKS

Sew 4 pieces cut with template 1, using different batik prints, to the sides of a 4½" batik square.

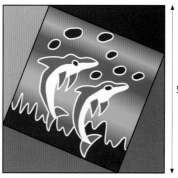

5¼"

Make 9.

Assembling the Quilt

Arrange and sew the blocks together into 3 rows of 3 blocks each. Join the rows.

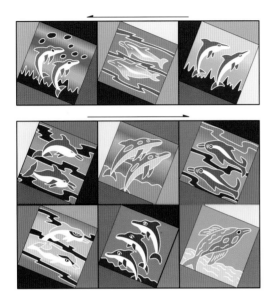

Adding the Borders

1. Referring to "Borders with Straight-Cut Corners" on page 102, measure and trim the 1⅞"-wide dark-batik inner borders and sew them to the quilt top.

2. To make the delectable mountains border, pair an 8" x 12" light batik piece with an 8" x 12" medium batik piece, right sides up. Referring to "Bias Squares" on page 16, cut and piece 1¾"-wide strips, and then cut 64 bias squares, 1½" x 1½".

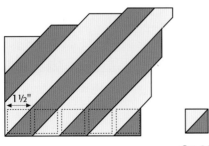

Cut 64.

3. Join 4 bias squares, 1 medium batik 1½" square, and 1 light 4⅛" triangle to make a delectable mountains unit.

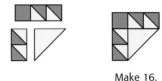

Make 16.

4. Join 3 medium batik 5½" triangles, 2 medium batik 6⅞" triangles, 4 delectable mountains units, and 5 light 1⅞" triangles to make each of 4 outer borders.

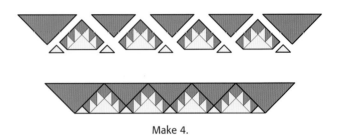

Make 4.

5. Referring to "Borders with Mitered Corners" on page 104, sew an outer border to each side of the quilt top and miter the corners.

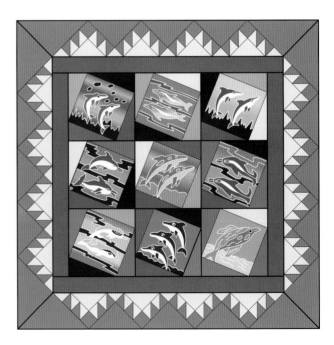

FINISHING THE QUILT

1. Layer the quilt top with batting and backing; baste and quilt as desired. *Quilting suggestion:* Outline-quilt the triangle surrounding the batik blocks and the figures in the batik squares. Quilt the borders in the ditch.

2. Referring to "Bias Binding" on page 107, cut and piece approximately 110" of bias binding and bind the edges of the quilt.

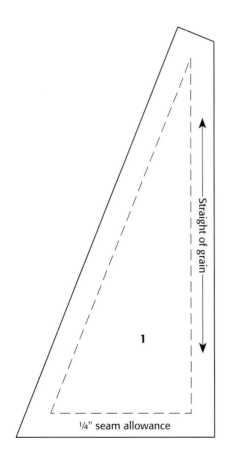

OTHER OPTION

LIGHTHOUSE LANDING
BY NANCY J. MARTIN, 2002, WOODINVILLE, WASHINGTON, 25" X 25". "LIGHTHOUSE LANDING" IS ANOTHER EXAMPLE OF A QUILT WITH THE TILT-A-WHIRL BLOCK AND THE DELECTABLE MOUNTAINS BORDER.

Dolly Madison's Amish Star

Dolly Madison's Amish Star by Nancy J. Martin, 1987, Woodinville, Washington, 62½" x 74½".
Quilted by Bev Payne, Lynnwood, Washington.

THIS QUILT IS *constructed as a bar quilt, which means that units are pieced and sewn into rows rather than into individual blocks. Solid colors create the look of an Amish quilt, which often uses several different shades of black in the same quilt. For visual interest, use the bright solid fabrics in the nine-patch unit of each block and a medium tone for the remainder of the Star block. The same-size bias squares in the Star blocks also appear in the double sawtooth border.*

MATERIALS

Yardage is based on 42"-wide fabric.

- 5 yds. total of assorted black solids for blocks and inner, middle, and outer plain borders
- ¼ yd. *each* of 12 assorted bright solids for blocks and first and second pieced borders
- ¼ yd. *each* of 12 assorted medium-tone solids for blocks and borders
- 4 yds. fabric for backing
- ⅝ yd. fabric for bias binding
- 66" x 78" piece of batting
- Bias Square ruler to cut bias squares

CUTTING

All measurements include ¼"-wide seam allowances.

From the assorted black solids, cut a total of:
- 7 strips, 4½" x 42"
- 6 strips, 2" x 42"
- 3 strips, 3⅞" x 42"
- 3 strips, 3½" x 42"
- 55 squares, 7" x 7"
- 12 squares, 5½" x 5½"; cut twice diagonally to yield 48 triangles

- 4 squares, 4¾" x 4¾" (unit 4)
- 10 pieces, 4¾" x 9" (unit 5)
- 6 squares, 9" x 9" (unit 6)
- 48 of template 1 (page 56)
- 48 squares, 2⅜" x 2⅜"; cut once diagonally to yield 96 triangles

From *each* of the 12 assorted bright solids, cut:
- 2 squares, 7" x 7" (24 total)
- 5 of template 1 (60 total, page 56)

From *each* of 7 medium-tone solids, cut:
- 3 squares, 7" x 7" (21 total)
- 8 squares, 2⅜" x 2⅜" (56 total); cut once diagonally to yield 112 triangles

From *each* of the remaining 5 medium-tone solids, cut:
- 2 squares, 7" x 7" (10 total)
- 8 squares, 2⅜" x 2⅜" (40 total); cut once diagonally to yield 80 triangles

ASSEMBLING THE QUILT

1. Pair each 7" black square with a 7" bright or medium-tone square, right sides up. Referring to "Bias Squares" on page 16, cut and piece 2"-wide strips and then cut 440 bias squares, 2" x 2". You will use 12 bias squares of each

color combination in the Star blocks. Save the remaining 296 bias squares for the sawtooth borders.

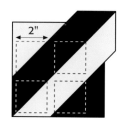

Cut 440.

2. Join 1 bias square and 2 matching 2⅜" triangles to make a star-tip unit. Make 8 matching units for each block.

Make 8 matching units for each block (total 96).

3. Join 1 bias square and 2 black 2⅜" triangles to make an inner-star unit. Make 4 matching units for each block.

Make 4 matching units for each block (total 48).

4. Join 4 black squares cut with template 1 and 5 matching bright-colored squares cut with template 1 to make unit 1.

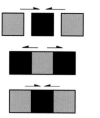

Unit 1
Make 12.

5. Join a 5½" black triangle, 2 star-tip units, and 1 inner-star unit from matching solids to make unit 2.

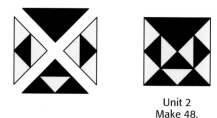

Unit 2
Make 48.

6. Referring to the color photo on page 52, arrange units 1, 2, 4, 5, and 6 as shown so that matching units form stars. Don't sew anything together yet.

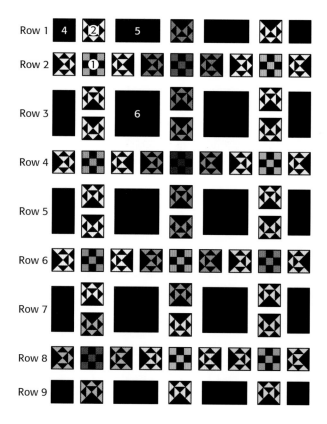

7. Now that you know the placement of the star colors, you can join unit 2s as shown to make unit 3.

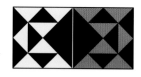

Unit 3

8. Join all the units and black pieces in horizontal rows. Join the rows.

ADDING THE BORDERS

Refer to the color photo on page 52 and the diagram below for the correct placement and positioning of each border.

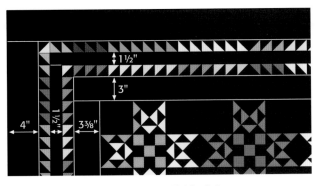

Measurements are finished sizes.

1. Referring to "Borders with Straight-Cut Corners" on page 102 and joining strips as needed, measure and trim the $3\frac{7}{8}$"-wide black inner borders and sew them to the sides of the quilt top. Then measure and trim the $3\frac{1}{2}$"-wide black inner borders and sew them to the top and bottom. The top should now measure $45\frac{1}{2}$" x $57\frac{1}{2}$", including seam allowances.

2. For first pieced borders, join 38 bias squares, 19 turned in each direction, to make each of 2 side sawtooth borders (as shown at right). Sew the borders to opposite sides of the quilt top. Then join 32 bias squares, 16 turned in each direction, to make each of the top and bottom sawtooth borders (as shown at right). Stitch these to the top and bottom of the quilt top.

3. Measure and trim the 2"-wide black middle borders and sew them to the quilt top as for the inner border. The top should now measure $51\frac{1}{2}$" x $63\frac{1}{2}$", including seam allowances.

4. For second pieced borders, join 42 bias squares, 21 turned in each direction, to make each of 2 side sawtooth borders. Sew the borders to opposite sides of the quilt top. Join 34 bias squares, 17 turned in each direction, adding a rotated bias square that forms a corner at each end, to make each of the top and bottom sawtooth borders. Stitch these to the top and bottom of the quilt as shown on page 56.

5. Measure and trim the $4\frac{1}{2}$"-wide black outer borders and sew them to the quilt top as for the inner and middle borders.

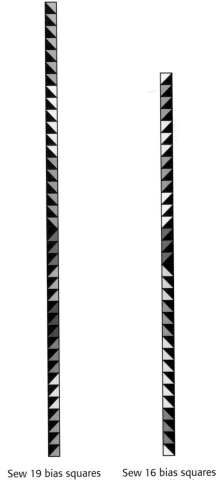

Sew 19 bias squares in each direction. Make 2.

Sew 16 bias squares in each direction. Make 2.

FINIƧHING THE QUILT

1. Layer the quilt top with batting and backing; baste and quilt as desired. *Quilting suggestion:* Quilt a traditional Amish pattern, the pumpkin seed, in the large black squares. Quilt a diagonal grid between the Star blocks and the first sawtooth border. Quilt a small cable pattern between the sawtooth borders and a fan pattern in the outer border.

2. Referring to "Bias Binding" on page 107, cut and piece approximately 280" of bias binding and bind the edges of the quilt.

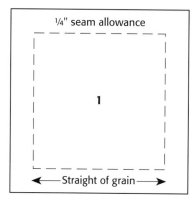

BLOSSOM BASKETS

BLOSSOM BASKETS BY NANCY J. MARTIN, 2001, WOODINVILLE, WASHINGTON, 65" x 65".
QUILTED BY MRS. ROY M. YODER, FREDERICKSBURG, OHIO.

THE DIAGONAL *setting of this quilt provides wonderful spaces in which to showcase a luscious floral print or other special fabric. The print is repeated in the wide border, which surrounds a pieced-triangle border. This border echoes the triangle pattern used in the Basket blocks and the triangles are a slightly smaller size than the basket triangles. The smaller-sized border was necessary so that an even number of units would fit into the required space, which meant the units could then change directions in the middle of the border to make an interesting border center and corners.*

MATERIALS

Yardage is based on 42"-wide fabric.

- ½ yd. *each* of 5 assorted yellow prints for blocks and middle border
- ½ yd. *each* of 5 assorted rose prints for blocks and middle border
- 2¼ yds. large-scale floral print for blocks, setting pieces, and outer border
- ⅝ yd. small-scale floral print for blocks
- ¼ yd. blue print for inner border
- 1 fat eighth *each* of 2 different blue prints for blocks
- 4 yds. fabric for backing
- ⅝ yd. fabric for bias binding
- 69" x 69" piece of batting
- Bias Square ruler to cut bias squares

CUTTING

All measurements include ¼"-wide seam allowances.

From the 5 assorted yellow prints, cut a total of:
- 19 squares, 8" x 8"

- 26 squares, 4⅝" x 4⅝"; cut once diagonally to yield 52 triangles
- 9 squares, 2½" x 2½"

From the 5 assorted rose prints, cut a total of:
- 19 squares, 8" x 8"
- 52 squares, 2¾" x 2¾"; cut once diagonally to yield 104 triangles

From the 2 blue prints for blocks, cut a total of:
- 5 squares, 4⅞" x 4⅞"; cut once diagonally to yield 10 triangles. You will have 1 triangle left over.
- 9 squares, 2⅞" x 2⅞"; cut once diagonally to yield 18 triangles

From the lengthwise grain of the large-scale floral print, cut:
- 4 strips, 6¼" x 68"
- 4 squares, 10½" x 10½"
- 5 squares, 4⅞" x 4⅞"; cut once diagonally to yield 10 triangles. You will have 1 triangle left over.
- 2 squares, 15½" x 15½"; cut twice diagonally to yield 8 side setting triangles
- 2 squares, 8" x 8"; cut once diagonally to yield 4 corner setting triangles

From the small-scale floral print, cut:

✦ 18 strips, 2½" x 6½"

✦ 5 squares, 4⅞" x 4⅞"; cut once diagonally to yield 10 triangles. You will have 1 triangle left over.

From the blue print for inner border, cut:

✦ 5 strips, 1¾" x 42"

MAKING THE BLOCKS

1. Pair 13 of the 8" yellow squares with 13 of the 8" rose squares, right sides facing up. Referring to "Bias Squares" on page 16, cut and piece 2½"-wide strips, and then cut 99 bias squares, 2½" x 2½".

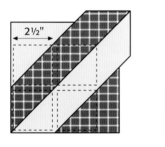

Cut 99.

2. Join 4 bias squares as shown to make each of units 1 and 2.

Unit 1
Make 9.

Unit 2
Make 9.

3. Join 3 bias squares and 1 yellow 2½" square to make unit 3.

Unit 3
Make 9.

4. Join a 4⅞" blue triangle and a 4⅞" large-scale floral triangle to make a basket base.

Make 9.

5. Join units 1, 2, and 3; a basket base; 2 small-scale floral 2½" x 6½" pieces; 2 blue 2⅞" triangles; and 1 small-scale floral 4⅞" triangle to make a block.

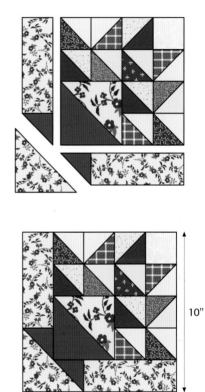

10"

Make 9.

Assembling the Quilt

1. Arrange and sew the Basket blocks, 10½" large-scale floral squares, and side setting triangles in diagonal rows. Join the rows. Add the corner setting triangles last.

2. Trim the outside edges and square up the corners of the quilt as necessary, leaving ¼" of fabric outside the block corners. The quilt should measure 43" x 43", including seam allowances.

Adding the Borders

1. Referring to "Borders with Straight-Cut Corners" on page 102 and joining strips as needed, measure and trim the 1¾"-wide blue inner borders and sew them to the quilt top. The quilt top should now measure 45½" x 45½", including seam allowances.

2. Pair the remaining 8" yellow and 8" rose squares, right sides up. Referring to "Bias Squares" on page 16, cut and piece 2½"-wide bias strips, and then cut 48 bias squares, 2⅜" x 2⅜". Resize the leftover bias squares from step 1 in "Making the Blocks" to 2⅜" x 2⅜", for a total of 52 bias squares.

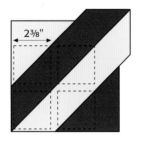

2⅜"

Cut 48.

3. Join 1 bias square, 2 rose triangles, and 1 yellow 4⅝" triangle to make a border unit.

Make 52.

4. Join 12 border units, changing direction in the center, for each of 4 middle borders.

Make 4.

5. Sew 2 middle borders to opposite sides of the quilt top. Sew a border unit to each end of the 2 remaining middle borders and add these to the top and bottom edges.

6. Measure and trim the 6¼"-wide floral outer borders and sew them to the quilt as for the inner border.

FINISHING THE QUILT

1. Layer the quilt top with batting and backing; baste and quilt as desired. *Quilting suggestion:* Quilt a medallion pattern in the setting squares and a partial medallion in the setting triangles. Quilt the Basket blocks in the ditch, and outline-quilt the large border triangles. Quilt a floral cable pattern in the outer border.

2. Referring to "Bias Binding" on page 107, cut and piece approximately 270" of bias binding and bind the edges of the quilt.

NURSERY RHYMES

NURSERY RHYMES BY NANCY J. MARTIN, 2001, WOODINVILLE, WASHINGTON, 47" X 59".
QUILTED BY MRS. EDWARD YODER, CLARK, MISSOURI.

THE LARGE *center in this block is a great place to feature one of the many juvenile or novelty prints that are now available. The on-point squares in the border repeat the lines of the blocks and the appliqué stars add the perfect finishing touch.*

MATERIALS

Yardage is based on 42"-wide fabric.

- 12 fat quarters of assorted bright prints for blocks and pieced border
- 1¼ yds. blue print for appliqué and outer border
- 1 yd. novelty print fabric for block centers*
- 3 yds. fabric for backing
- ½ yd. fabric for bias binding
- 51" x 63" piece of batting

Additional yardage may be needed to fussy cut the squares (see page 6).

CUTTING

All measurements include ¼"-wide seam allowances.

From the 12 assorted bright prints, cut a total of:
- 12 squares, 7¼" x 7¼"; cut twice diagonally to yield 48 triangles
- 24 squares, 6⅞" x 6⅞"; cut once diagonally to yield 48 triangles
- 60 squares, 2⅝" x 2⅝"

From the novelty print, fussy cut:
- 12 squares, 6½" x 6½"

From the blue print, cut:
- 6 strips, 2¾" x 42"
- 6 of template 1 (page 65)

- 29 squares, 4¼" x 4¼"; cut twice diagonally to yield 116 triangles
- 4 squares, 2⅜" x 2⅜"; cut once diagonally to yield 8 triangles

ASSEMBLING THE QUILT

1. Sew 4 matching 7¼" bright triangles to the sides of a 6½" novelty print square. Then sew 4 matching 6⅞" bright triangles to each side to complete a block.

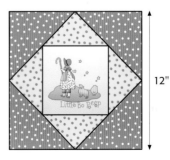

Make 12.

2. Arrange and sew the blocks into 4 rows of 3 blocks each. Join the rows.

3. Using your favorite method and referring to the color photo on page 62, appliqué the blue stars cut with template 1 to the intersections where the quilt blocks meet. Position the stars at random angles.

ADDING THE BORDERS

1. Join 12 bright 2⅝" squares, 22 blue 4¼" triangles, and 2 blue 2⅜" triangles to make each of the pieced top and bottom borders. Join 16 bright 2⅝" squares and 32 blue 4¼" triangles for each pieced side border.

Top and Bottom Border
Make 2.

Side Border
Make 2.

2. Sew the pieced top and bottom borders to the quilt top, and then add the pieced side borders.

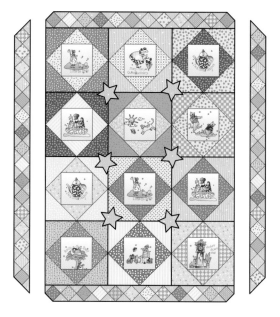

3. Join 1 bright 2⅝" square, 2 blue 4¼" triangles, and 1 blue 2⅜" triangle to make a corner triangle. Add to the corners of the quilt top.

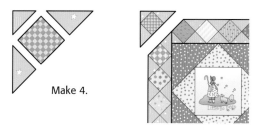

Make 4.

4. Referring to "Borders with Straight-Cut Corners" on page 102 and joining strips as needed, measure and trim the 2¾"-wide blue outer borders and sew them to the quilt top.

FINISHING THE QUILT

1. Layer the quilt top with batting and backing; baste and quilt as desired. *Quilting suggestion:*

Outline-quilt the motifs in the novelty print and the inner triangles of the blocks. Quilt a circular pattern in the triangles behind the stars and a half-circle pattern in the setting triangles. Outline-quilt the on-point squares in the pieced border, and quilt a small cable pattern in the outer border.

2. Referring to "Bias Binding" on page 107, cut and piece approximately 225" of bias binding and bind the edges of the quilt.

OTHER OPTIONS

This pattern lends itself to a variety of center motifs and sizes. The following chart includes some of the most commonly used sizes. Refer to the diagram below the chart for piece placement.

Finished Block	Center Squares	Squares for Small Triangles	Squares for Large Triangles	Border Squares	Squares for Small Border Triangles	Squares for Large Border Triangles
	(A)	(B)	(C)	(D)	(E)	(F)
6"	3½"	4¾" ⊠	3⅞" ◩	1⁹⁄₁₆"	1⅝" ◩	2¾" ⊠
8"	4½"	5¼" ⊠	4⅞" ◩	1⁹⁄₁₆"	1⅞" ◩	3¼" ⊠
9"	5"	5¾" ⊠	5⅜" ◩	2⅛"	2" ◩	3½" ⊠
10"	5½"	6¼" ⊠	5⅞" ◩	2¼"	2⅛" ◩	3¾" ⊠
12"	6½"	7¼" ⊠	6⅞" ◩	2⅝"	2⅜" ◩	4¼" ⊠

◩ = Cut squares once diagonally.

⊠ = Cut squares twice diagonally.

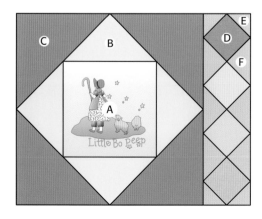

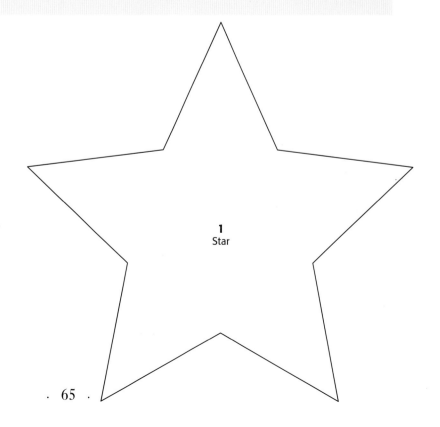

1
Star

CHILDHOOD DAZE

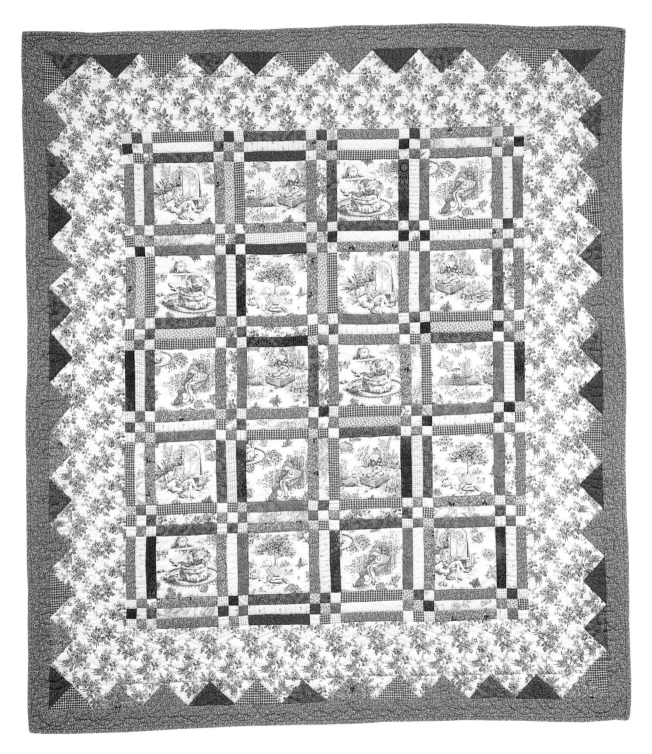

CHILDHOOD DAZE BY NANCY J. MARTIN AND CLEO NOLLETTE, 2001, WOODINVILLE, WASHINGTON, 58" X 67".
QUILTED BY LAVINA SCHWARTZ, HILLSDALE, OHIO.

THE LOVELY, *soft, blue-and-white colors in this quilt remind me of the hazy, happy days of childhood. A variety of blue-print strips border an enchanting novelty print. The wide light-print border creates a restful space between the blocks and the pieced border. An outer border anchors the pieced border and completes the design.*

MATERIALS

Yardage is based on 42"-wide fabric.

- ⅜ yd. *each* of 6 assorted medium blue prints for sashing and middle border
- 1½ yds. light background print for inner and middle borders
- ¼ yd. *each* of 6 assorted light background prints for sashing
- 1 yd. novelty print fabric for block centers*
- ¾ yd. medium blue print for outer border
- 3½ yds. fabric for backing
- ⅝ yd. fabric for bias binding
- 61" x 70" piece of batting

*Additional yardage may be needed to fussy cut the squares (see page 6).

MIXING IT UP

Vary the fabrics in each strip set as they are sewn together. Select a different combination for each strip set and vary the position of the fabric within the strip sets.

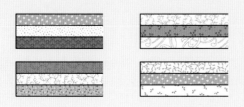

CUTTING

All measurements include ¼"-wide seam allowances.

From the 6 assorted medium blue prints, cut a total of:
- 22 strips, 1½" x 42"
- 1 strip, 1½" x 14"
- 13 squares, 5¾" x 5¾"; cut twice diagonally to yield 52 triangles

From the 6 assorted light background prints for sashing, cut a total of:
- 14 strips, 1½" x 42"
- 2 strips, 1½" x 14"

From the novelty print, fussy cut:
- 20 squares, 6½" x 6½"

From the lengthwise grain of the light background print for borders, cut:
- 4 strips, 5¾" x 52"
- 12 squares, 5¾" x 5¾"; cut twice diagonally to yield 48 triangles

From the medium blue print for outer border, cut:
- 7 strips, 2¼" x 42"

MAKING THE BLOCKS

1. Join 2 medium blue 1½" x 42" strips and 1 light background 1½" x 42" strip as shown to make a strip set. Make 10 strip sets. From the strip sets, cut 49 segments, each 6½" wide. Crosscut the remaining strip sets into 30 segments, each 1½" wide.

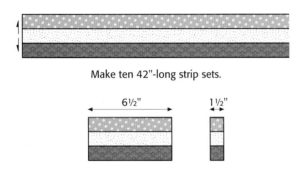

Make ten 42"-long strip sets.

6½"   1½"

2. Join 2 light background 1½" x 42" strips and 1 medium blue 1½" x 42" strip as shown to make each of 2 strip sets. Make another strip set in the same manner with the 1½" x 14" light background and medium blue strips. From the strip sets, cut 60 segments, each 1½" wide.

Make two 42"-long strip sets and one 14"-long strip set.

1½"

Cut 60.

3. Join one 1½"-wide segment from step 1 and 2 segments from step 2 as shown to make a nine-patch unit.

Make 30.

ASSEMBLING THE QUILT

Arrange and sew 4 novelty-print 6½" squares and 5 medium and light background 6½"-wide segments into each of 5 rows. Sew 5 nine-patch units and 4 medium and light background 6½"-wide segments into each of 6 rows. Join the rows.

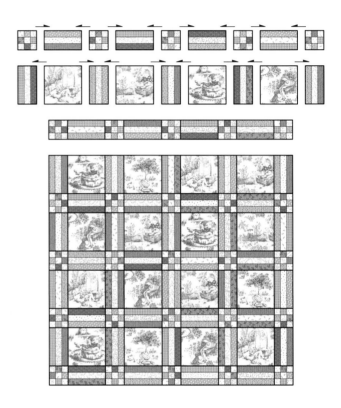

ADDING THE BORDERS

1. Referring to "Borders with Straight-Cut Corners" on page 102, measure and trim the 5¾"-wide light background inner borders and sew them to the quilt top.

2. Stitch together 11 light background triangles and 12 medium blue triangles to make each of the top and bottom middle borders. Stitch together 13 light background triangles and 14 medium blue triangles to make each of the side middle borders.

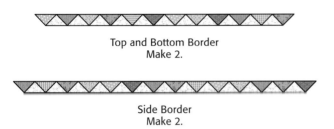

Top and Bottom Border
Make 2.

Side Border
Make 2.

3. Referring to "Borders with Mitered Corners" on page 104, sew the middle borders to the quilt top and miter the corners.

4. Joining strips as needed, measure and trim the 2¼"-wide outer borders and sew them to the quilt as for the inner border.

FINISHING THE QUILT

1. Layer the quilt top with batting and backing; baste and quilt as desired. *Quilting suggestion:* Outline-quilt the motifs in the novelty print. Quilt the sashing and sashing squares in the ditch. Quilt a trellis pattern in the wide border, and a loop pattern in the pieced border and outer border.

2. Referring to "Bias Binding" on page 107, cut and piece approximately 270" of bias binding and bind the edges of the quilt.

CABIN IN THE TREES

QUILTS WITH OTHER PIECED BORDERS

CABIN IN THE TREES BY NANCY J. MARTIN AND CLEO NOLLETTE, 2001, WOODINVILLE, WASHINGTON, 46½" x 46½". QUILTED BY CLARA YODER, KENTON, OHIO.

THE TREE *border in this quilt surrounds the Church, Tree, and Cabin blocks. The tree border would also be a perfect frame for any quilt with a wildlife or outdoor theme.*

MATERIALS

Yardage is based on 42"-wide fabric.

- 1¾ yds. light print for blocks, sashing, and borders
- 6 fat quarters of assorted green prints for trees
- ⅜ yd. red print for blocks and star centers
- ¼ yd. red check for doors and windows
- 1 fat quarter of green print for roofs and steeple
- 1 fat eighth of yellow print for star tips
- 1 fat eighth of brown for tree trunks
- 3 yds. fabric for backing
- ½ yd. fabric for bias binding
- 51" x 51" piece of batting
- Bias Square ruler to cut bias squares

CUTTING

All measurements include ¼"-wide seam allowances.

From the light print, cut:
- 5 strips, 2½" x 42", for outer borders
- 4 strips, 3" x 34½", for horizontal sashing
- 12 pieces, 3" x 8½", for vertical sashing
- 2 squares, 7" x 7", for bias squares
- 11 pieces, 2" x 3" (A)
- 10 pieces, 1½" x 2" (B)
- 5 pieces, 2½" x 3" (D1)
- 1 piece, 3" x 5½" (D2)

- 12 pieces, 1½" x 2", for large Tree blocks
- 6 and 6 reversed of template 2 (page 76) for large Tree blocks
- 4 strips, 2" x 18", for small tree border
- 8 pieces, 1" x 1¼", for small tree border
- 16 of template 3 (page 76) for small tree border
- 4 and 4 reversed of template 4 (page 76) for small tree border
- 4 squares, 3¼" x 3¼"; cut twice diagonally to yield 16 triangles for stars
- 16 squares, 1½" x 1½", for stars

From the red print, cut:
- 5 strips, 1½" x 42", for cabin siding
- 2 squares, 7" x 7", for bias squares
- 10 pieces, 2" x 2" (C1)
- 1 piece, 2" x 2¼" (C2)
- 6 pieces, 1½" x 3½" (F)
- 12 pieces, 1½" x 5½" (G)
- 4 squares, 2½" x 2½", for star centers

From the red check, cut:
- 3 strips, 1½" x 42", for doors and windows

From the assorted green prints, cut:
- Assorted widths from 1" to 2½" of 21"-long strips (see "Making the Tree Blocks" on page 73 and "Adding the Borders" on page 74)

From the green print for roofs and steeple, cut:
- 2 squares, 7" x 7", for bias squares
- 6 pieces, 2" x 4" (E)

From the yellow print, cut:

✦ 16 squares, 1⅞" x 1⅞"; cut once diagonally to yield 32 triangles for stars

From the brown, cut:

✦ 6 squares, 1½" x 1½", for large Tree blocks

✦ 4 strips, 1" x 18", for small tree border

✦ 4 squares, 1" x 1", for small tree border

MAKING THE CABIN AND CHURCH BLOCKS

1. Pair a 7" light square with a 7" red-print square, right sides up. Referring to "Bias Squares" on page 16, cut and piece 2"-wide strips, and then cut 6 bias squares, 2" x 2". Repeat, pairing a 7" green square with a 7" red square. Repeat, pairing a 7" green square with a 7" light square. Cut 2 additional bias squares, 1¼" x 1¼", from the remainder of the green and light pieced fabric.

Cut 6.

Cut 6.

1¼"

Cut 6.   Cut 2.

2. Join 1 of each color combination of bias square and pieces A, B, C1, D1, and E to make the upper section of a cabin.

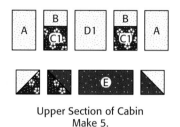

Upper Section of Cabin
Make 5.

3. Join 1 of each color combination of 2" bias square, two 1¼" bias squares, and pieces A, C2, D2, and E to make the upper section of the church.

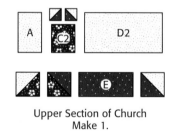

Upper Section of Church
Make 1.

4. Join 2 red-print 1½" x 42" strips and 1 red-check 1½" x 42" strip to make a strip set. From the strip set, cut 6 segments, each 3½" wide, for the door unit.

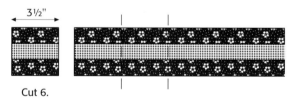

3½"

Cut 6.

5. Join 3 red-print 1½" x 42" strips and 2 red-check 1½" x 42" strips to make a strip set. From the strip set, cut 6 segments, each 2½" wide, for the window unit.

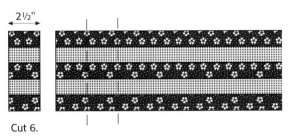

Cut 6.

6. Join a door unit, window unit, and pieces F and G to make the lower section of the Cabin and Church blocks.

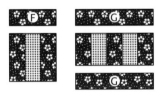

7. Join the upper and lower sections of the church and cabins.

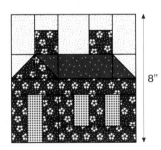

8"

Cabin Block
Make 5.

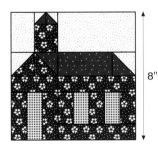

8"

Church Block
Make 1.

MAKING THE TREE BLOCKS

1. Sew together assorted 21"-long green strips in various widths from 1" to 2½" on their long edges, to make a piece of yardage approximately 16" wide and 21" long. Use template 1 (page 76) to cut 6 trees from the pieced yardage.

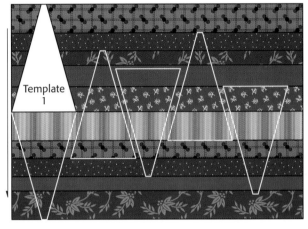

Template 1

Cut 6.

2. Join 1 tree (template 1), 2 light pieces (template 2 and template 2 reversed), 1 brown 1½" square, and 2 light 1½" x 2" pieces to make a large Tree block.

2   2r

Make 6.

Assembling the Quilt

Arrange and sew the Cabin blocks, Church block, Tree blocks, and 8½" vertical sashing strips as shown to make 3 horizontal rows. Join the rows of blocks with 34½"-long horizontal sashing strips between the rows and at the top and bottom edges.

Holding On

A good habit to develop is to use a seam ripper or long pin to guide the fabric gently up to the needle. You can hold seam intersections together or make minor adjustments before the fabric is sewn.

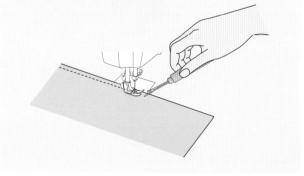

Adding the Borders

1. Sew assorted 1"- to 1¾"-wide green strips to make yardage for the small trees. You'll need 1 piece of yardage approximately 25" wide and 21" long. Cut 68 of template 3 (page 76) from the strip-pieced yardage.

    NOTE: *You can also cut some of the trees from plain green fabric, as I did, to add variety.*

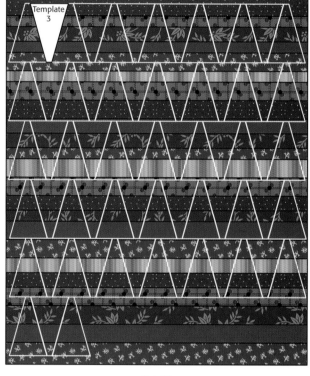

Cut 68.

2. Join 17 trees (template 3) and 16 light pieces (template 3) as shown to make each of 4 rows of trees. Add light pieces (template 4 and template 4 reversed) to the ends of each row.

Make 4.

3. Join 4 brown 1" x 18" strips, alternating with 4 light 2" x 18" strips to make a strip set. From the strip set, cut 16 segments, each 1" wide.

1"

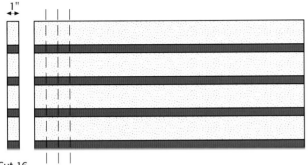

Cut 16.

4. Starting with a brown square at the left-hand end, join 4 segments from step 3 end to end. Add a 1" brown square to the right-hand end, and a 1" x 1¼" light piece to each end to make each of 4 rows of trunks. Sew a row of trees to a row of trunks to make 4 pieced borders.

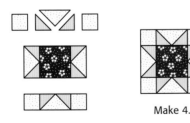

5. Sew a tree border to opposite sides of the quilt top.

6. Join 1 red-print 2½" square, 4 light 3¼" triangles, 8 yellow triangles, and 4 light 1½" squares to make a Star block for the corners.

Make 4.

7. Sew a Star block to each end of the remaining tree borders. Add these to the top and bottom edges.

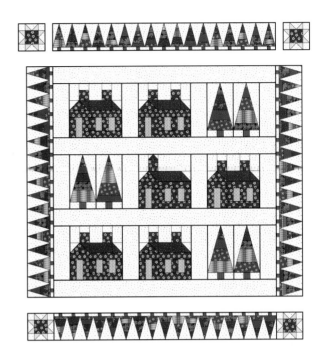

8. Referring to "Borders with Straight-Cut Corners" on page 102 and joining strips as needed, measure and trim the 2½"-wide light-print outer borders and sew them to the quilt top.

FINISHING THE QUILT

1. Layer the quilt top with batting and backing; baste and quilt as desired. *Quilting suggestion:* Outline-quilt the pieces in the Church block, Cabin blocks, and large and small Tree blocks. Quilt a cable pattern in the inner sashing pieces. Quilt a delicate crescent and diamond pattern in the outer border.

2. Referring to "Bias Binding" on page 107, cut and piece approximately 200" of bias binding and bind the edges of the quilt.

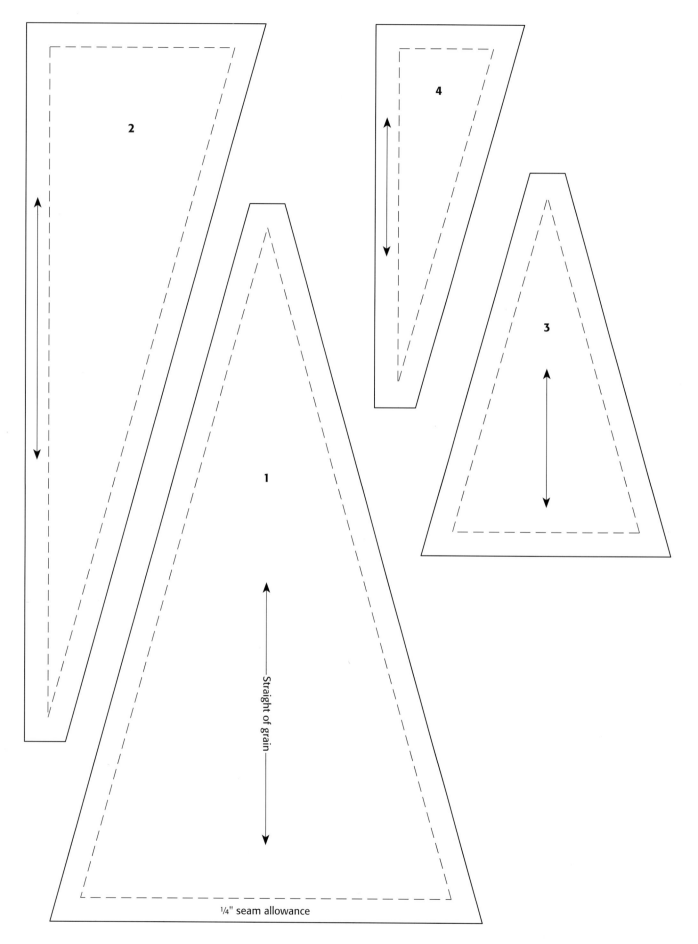

2

4

1

3

Straight of grain

¼" seam allowance

54-40 or Fight

54-40 OR FIGHT BY NANCY J. MARTIN, 2001, WOODINVILLE, WASHINGTON, 60½" x 60½".
QUILTED BY MRS. MENNO MILLER, NAVARRE, OHIO.

B IAS RECTANGLES *are used to make the lively red stars in this quilt. They are also used in the energizing border, which repeats the sharp points of the stars and creates an effective frame. This is another example where an even number of units is required for the borders so that the units can change direction in the middle of each border and create a pleasing corner design (see "Patchwork Borders" on page 11).*

MATERIALS

Yardage is based on 42"-wide fabric.

+ 1⅛ yd. *each* of 4 light prints for blocks, sashing strips, and border
+ 1½ yds. dark red print for stars
+ 4 fat quarters of assorted dark green prints for blocks and sashing
+ 4 fat quarters of assorted medium green prints for blocks and sashing squares
+ ¾ yd. dark green print A for border
+ ¾ yd. dark green print B for border
+ 3⅞ yds. fabric for backing
+ ½ yd. fabric for bias binding
+ 65" x 65" piece of batting
+ BiRangle ruler to cut bias rectangles

CUTTING

All measurements include ¼"-wide seam allowances.

From the dark red print, cut:
+ 4 pieces, 12" x 42"

From the 4 light prints, cut a total of:
+ 8 pieces, 12" x 42"
+ 60 strips, 2" x 9½"

+ 20 strips, 2" x 21"
+ 4 squares, 3½" x 3½"

From the assorted medium green fat eighths, cut a total of:
+ 16 strips, 2" x 21"
+ 18 squares, 2" x 2"

From the assorted dark green fat eighths, cut a total of:
+ 16 strips, 2" x 21"
+ 18 squares, 2" x 2"

From dark green print A, cut:
+ 2 pieces, 12" x 42"

From dark green print B, cut:
+ 2 pieces, 12" x 42"

MAKING THE BLOCKS

1. Pair each dark red 12" x 42" piece with a light 12" x 42" piece, right sides up. Referring to "Bias Rectangles" on page 17, cut and piece 2½"-wide strips, and then cut 200 bias rectangles, 2" x 3½". You'll need 100 with the red on the right and 100 with the red on the left.

Make 100.   Make 100.

2. Sew a 2" x 21" medium green strip to a 2" x 21" light strip as shown to make a strip set. Make 10 strip sets. Layer 2 different sets of strips on top of each other. From each set of strips, cut 10 segments, each 2" wide.

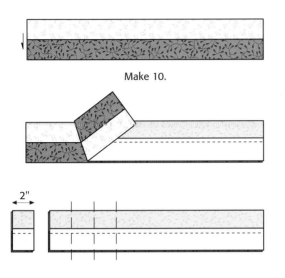

Make 10.

2"

3. Join the pairs of segments to make 50 four-patch units.

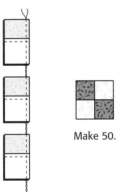

Make 50.

4. Repeat steps 2 and 3 to make 50 four-patch units from 2" x 21" light strips and dark green strips, and 25 four-patch units from 2" x 21" medium green strips and dark green strips.

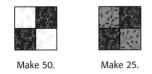

Make 50.   Make 25.

5. Referring to the diagram below, join 8 bias rectangles, 1 medium green and dark green four-patch unit, 2 matching light and medium green four-patch units, and 2 matching light and dark green four-patch units to make a block. Make sure the dark green squares form a diagonal chain in one direction, and the medium green squares form a diagonal chain in the opposite direction.

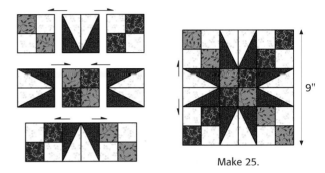

9"

Make 25.

ASSEMBLING THE QUILT

Arrange the blocks, sashing strips, and sashing squares so that the dark green squares form a continuous diagonal chain, and the medium green squares form another continuous diagonal chain. This will determine the color of the sashing square that links the chain. Keeping the arranged order, sew the rows of blocks and rows of sashing pieces together. Join the rows.

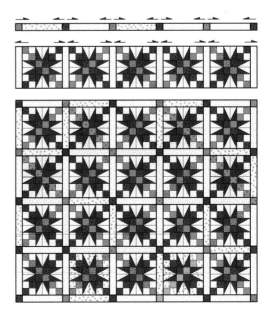

ADDING THE BORDER

1. Pair a 12" x 42" light piece with a 12" x 42" dark green print A piece, right sides up. Referring to "Bias Rectangles" on page 17, cut and piece 2½"-wide strips, and then cut 72 bias rectangles, 2" x 3½". You'll need 36 with dark green A on the left and 36 with dark green A on the right. Repeat with pieces of light and dark green print B to make 72 bias rectangles. You'll need 36 with dark green B on the left and 36 with dark green B on the right.

Make 36 each using dark green print A.   Make 36 each using dark green print B.

2. Alternating dark green prints A and B, join 36 bias rectangles, placing 18 points in each direction, for each of 4 borders.

Make 4.

3. Sew borders to opposite sides of the quilt top. Add a light-print corner square to each end of the 2 remaining borders and add these strips to the top and bottom edges of the quilt top.

FINISHING THE QUILT

1. Layer the quilt top with batting and backing; baste and quilt as desired. *Quilting suggestion:* Quilt the blocks in the ditch, and quilt a small cable pattern in the sashing strips.

2. Referring to "Bias Binding" on page 107, cut and piece approximately 255" of bias binding and bind the edges of the quilt.

WAGON TRACKS

WAGON TRACKS BY NANCY J. MARTIN AND CLEO NOLLETTE, 2001, WOODINVILLE, WASHINGTON, 62½" x 62½". QUILTED BY MARY CHRISTNER, BERN, INDIANA.

W AGON TRACKS *is similar to blocks called Jacob's Ladder, Stepping Stones, Golden Stairs, and Underground Railroad. The distinguishing element in the Wagon Tracks block is its coloration. The large triangles are made from the darkest and lightest fabrics, while the medium fabrics form a chain across the quilt. The large dark triangles continue into the border, completing the design and making a graceful border treatment.*

MATERIALS

Yardage is based on 42"-wide fabric.

- ½ yd. *each* of 7 assorted light prints for blocks
- 7 fat quarters of assorted dark prints (purple, burgundy, brown, and black) for blocks and border
- 6 fat quarters of assorted medium prints (pink, green, and blue) for blocks
- 1 yd. blue print for border
- 4 yds. fabric for backing
- ½ yd. fabric for bias binding
- 67" x 67" piece of batting

CUTTING

All measurements include ¼"-wide seam allowances.

From the 7 assorted light prints, cut a total of:
- 72 squares, 3⅞" x 3⅞"; cut once diagonally to yield 144 triangles
- 36 strips, 2" x 21"

From the 7 assorted dark prints, cut a total of:
- 72 squares, 3⅞" x 3⅞"; cut once diagonally to yield 144 triangles
- 24 squares, 3½" x 3½"

From the 6 assorted medium prints, cut a total of:
- 36 strips, 2" x 21"

From the blue print, cut:
- 4 pieces, 4½" x 9½"
- 4 pieces, 4½" x 13½"
- 8 pieces, 4½" x 18½"

MAKING THE BLOCKS

1. Sew each light triangle to a dark triangle.

Make 144.

2. Using different combinations of fabric, sew a light strip to a medium strip as shown to make 36 strip sets. Layer 2 sets of strips on top of each other. From each set of strips, cut 10 segments, each 2" wide.

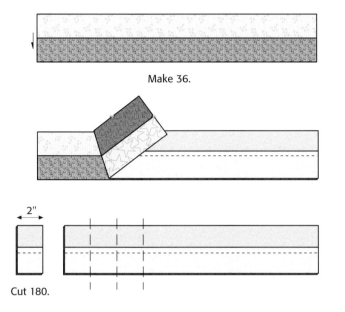

Make 36.

Cut 180.

3. Join pairs of segments to make 180 four-patch units, using different combinations of fabric.

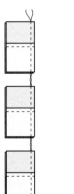

Make 180.

4. Join 5 four-patch units and 4 pieced triangles to make a block.

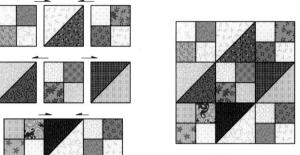

9"

Make 36.

Assembling the Quilt

Arrange and sew the blocks into 6 rows of 6 blocks each, rotating the blocks as needed to form the design.

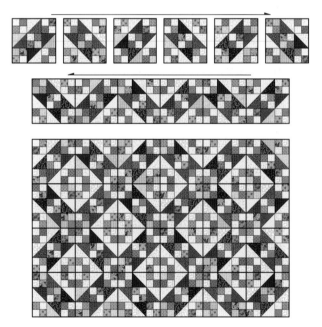

ADDING THE BORDER

1. With a white or yellow pencil, draw a diagonal line on the wrong side of the 3½" dark squares. Place a square on one end of a 4½" x 9½" blue piece, right sides together. Stitch on the drawn line. Trim the excess fabric, leaving a ¼" seam allowance. Make 2 with triangles in the upper right corner and 2 with triangles in the upper left corner.

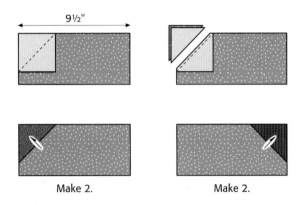

Make 2.   Make 2.

2. Repeat step 1 to make two 13½" pieces with triangles in the upper right corner and two with triangles in the upper left corner. Make eight 18½" pieces with triangles at each end.

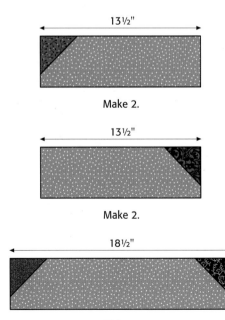

Make 2.

Make 2.

Make 8.

3. Join the border pieces as shown to make 2 borders for the sides and 2 borders for the top and bottom.

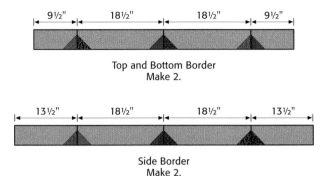

Top and Bottom Border
Make 2.

Side Border
Make 2.

4. Referring to the color photo on page 81, sew the side borders to opposite sides of the quilt top, and then add the top and bottom borders.

   Take care to align the dark triangles in the borders with the dark triangles in the quilt top to extend the design into the borders.

FINISHING THE QUILT

1. Layer the quilt top with batting and backing; baste and quilt as desired. *Quilting suggestion:* Quilt each block in the ditch. Quilt a feather pattern in the border.

2. Referring to "Bias Binding" on page 107, cut and piece approximately 260" of bias binding and bind the edges of the quilt.

SETTING STARS

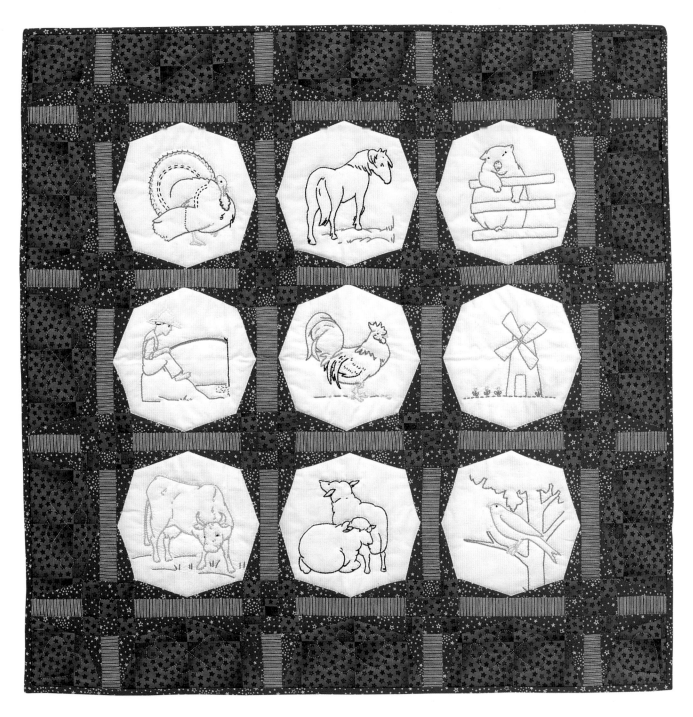

STARS IN THE BARNYARD BY NANCY J. MARTIN, 2001, WOODINVILLE, WASHINGTON, 36½" x 36½".
QUILTED BY ALVINA NELSON, SALINA, KANSAS. FROM THE COLLECTION OF BETH KOVICH.

THIS SETTING *is great for framing a novelty print or an embroidered block. The long triangles reduce the amount of white space in the block corners and form an elongated star pattern when combined with more blocks and sashing. Half blocks and quarter blocks along the outside edges continue the star pattern and form the border.*

MATERIALS

Yardage is based on 42"-wide fabric.

- ⁷⁄₈ yd. deep blue print for block corners and border half blocks
- ¾ yd. novelty print or 9 embroidered blocks at least 8½" x 8½" for block centers*
- ¾ yd. red print for star tips and sashing
- ⅜ yd. blue stripe for sashing
- 1¼ yds. fabric for backing
- ⅜ yd. for fabric bias binding
- 41" x 41" piece of batting

*Additional yardage may be needed to fussy cut the squares if using a novelty print (see page 6).

CUTTING

All measurements include ¼"-wide seam allowances.

From the deep blue print, cut:
- 80 squares, 1½" x 1½"
- 12 of template 2 (page 90)
- 4 of template 3 (page 89)

From the red print, cut:
- 64 and 64 reversed of template 4 (page 90)
- 64 squares, 1½" x 1½"

From the novelty-print or embroidered blocks, cut:
- 9 of template 1 (page 89)

From the blue stripe, cut:
- 24 strips, 1½" x 6½"
- 16 strips, 1½" x 3½"

MAKING THE BLOCKS

1. Sew a deep blue square to the end of each piece cut with template 4 reversed as shown.

Make 64.

2. Sew a piece cut with template 4 to one side of the center block. Sew a unit from step 1 to the adjacent side of the block. Start stitching at the edge of the square, pivot at the corner, and continue to the end of the piece. Repeat all around the angled edges of the block.

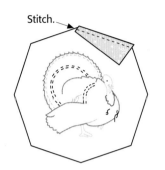

Stitch.

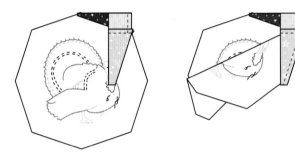

Stitch to seam, pivoting at corner, and stitch to end.

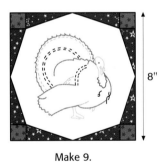

8"

Make 9.

3. Following the procedure in step 2, make a half block using pieces cut with template 2.

Half Block
Make 12.

4. Following the procedure in step 2, make a corner block using pieces cut with template 3.

Corner Block
Make 4.

Assembling the Quilt

1. Sew a red square to each end of a 6½"-long blue-stripe piece to make a sashing strip.

Make 24.

2. Join 3 blocks, 4 sashing strips, and 2 half blocks to make each of 3 block rows.

Make 3.

3. Sew a red square to one end of a 3½"-long blue-stripe piece to make a border sashing strip. Join 2 corner blocks, 3 half blocks, and 4 border sashing strips to make each of the top and bottom rows.

Make 16.

Make 2.

4. Join 2 border sashing strips, 3 sashing strips, and 4 deep blue squares to make each of 4 sashing rows.

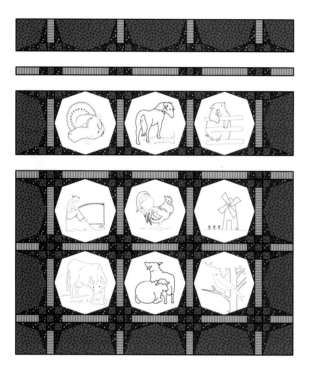

Make 4.

5. Join rows of blocks, sashing rows, and top and bottom rows.

FINISHING THE QUILT

1. Layer the quilt top with batting and backing; baste and quilt as desired. *Quilting suggestion:* Outline-quilt the embroidered motifs. Quilt the star points and sashing strips in the ditch. Quilt a small heart pattern in the half and corner blocks.

2. Referring to "Bias Binding" on page 107, cut and piece approximately 160" of bias binding and bind the edges of the quilt.

SECOND TIME AROUND

Incorporate used linens or embroidered blocks in your project only if the fabric is firmly woven and shows no weak or worn areas from use, embroidery stitches are secure and all knots are firmly in place, and lace trims and edgings are intact.

Don't hesitate to purchase stained or torn linens for your projects. If you cannot remove the stains, cover them with embroidery stitches. The following stain removal tips may prove helpful:

1. Treat stains on used linens individually. Do not wash with other items.

2. Never use chlorine bleach or oxalic acid.

3. Sodium perborate, available at drugstores, will remove some stains and mildew.

4. Treat rust stains with a paste made from baking soda.

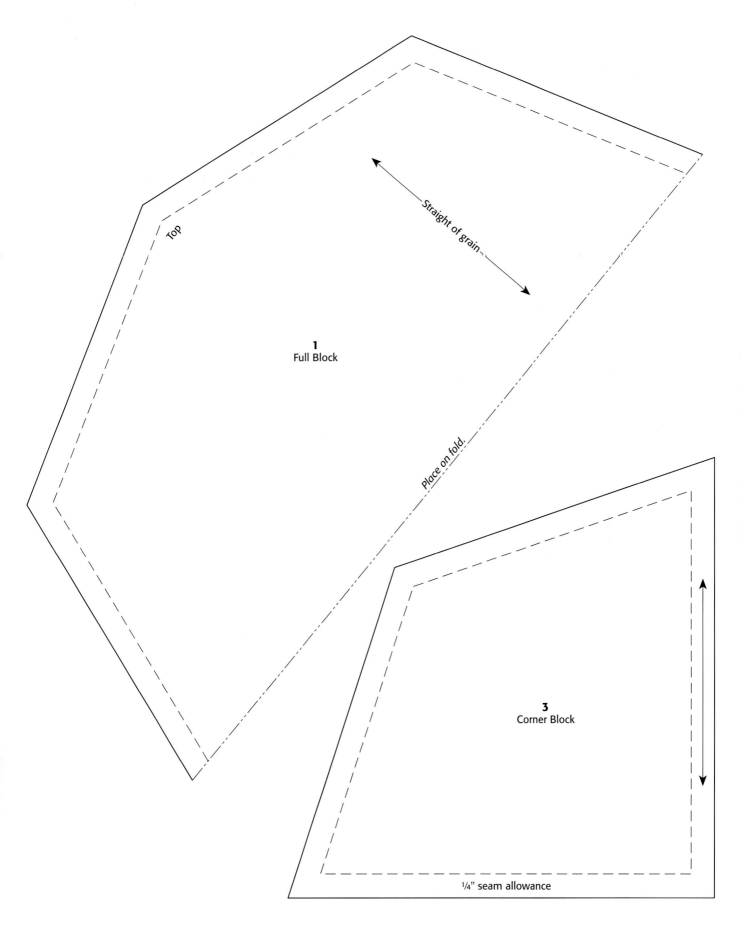

1
Full Block

Top

Straight of grain

Place on fold.

3
Corner Block

¼" seam allowance

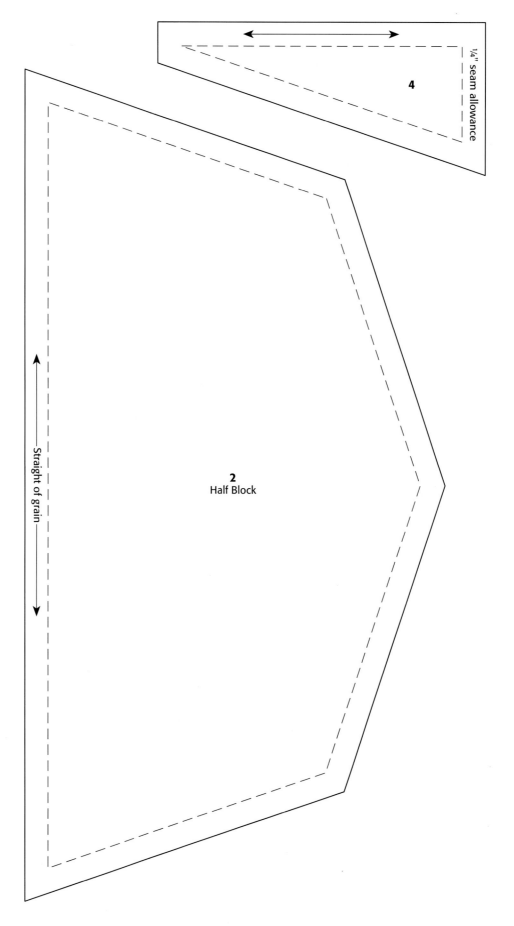

¼" seam allowance

4

Straight of grain

2
Half Block

HEARTS AND FLOWERS

HEARTS AND FLOWERS BY NANCY J. MARTIN, 2001, WOODINVILLE, WASHINGTON, 48½" x 60½".
QUILTED BY FRANKIE SCHMITT, KENMORE, WASHINGTON.

THE APPLIQUÉ *border adds a light touch to these colorful Heart blocks. Strip piecing and bias squares speed up the assembly of the blocks. Although appliqué borders may seem time-consuming, using just a portion of an appliqué border in two opposite corners of the quilt quickly moves the process along. A border like this also eliminates the need to plan a new appliqué curve design when working on a quilt with a different length and width from the one shown.*

MATERIALS

Yardage is based on 42"-wide fabric.

- ¾ yd. *each* of 6 assorted light prints for blocks and border
- ½ yd. *each* of 7 assorted red prints for blocks
- ¾ yd. red print for bias-strip appliqué and bias binding
- 3 yds. fabric for backing
- 53" x 65" piece of batting
- 18 buttons, 1½" diameter, for flower centers
- Bias Square ruler to cut bias squares

CUTTING

All measurements include ¼"-wide seam allowances.

From the assorted light prints, cut a total of:
- 32 squares, 6½" x 6½"
- 15 squares, 7" x 7"
- 44 strips, 2" x 21"
- 24 squares, 2" x 2"

From the assorted red prints, cut a total of:
- 15 squares, 7" x 7"
- 26 strips, 2" x 21"
- 40 of template 1 (page 95)

- 18 of template 2 (page 95)
- 1 and 1 reversed of template 3 (page 95)

MAKING THE BLOCKS

1. Pair the 7" light squares with the 7" red squares, right sides up. Referring to "Bias Squares" on page 16, cut and piece 2"-wide strips, and then cut 120 bias squares, 2" x 2".

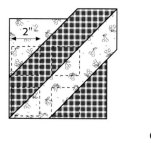

Cut 120.

2. Join 2 red strips to make strip set 1. Make 3 strip sets. From the strip sets, cut 24 segments, each 2" wide.

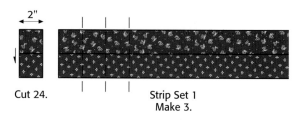

Cut 24.   Strip Set 1
Make 3.

3. Join 4 red strips to make strip set 2. Make 5 strip sets. From the strip sets, cut 48 segments, each 2" wide.

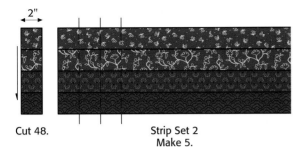

Cut 48.   Strip Set 2
                       Make 5.

4. Join 2 light strips to make strip set 3. Make 3 strip sets. From the strip sets, cut 24 segments, each 2" wide.

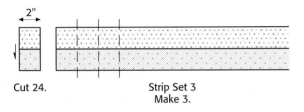

Cut 24.   Strip Set 3
                       Make 3.

5. Join 1 segment from strip set 1, 2 segments from strip set 2, and 1 segment from strip set 3; 5 bias squares; and 1 light 2" square to make the left half of a Heart block. Repeat to make the right half of a Heart block.

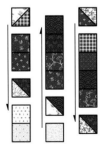
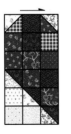

Left Half
Make 12.

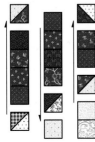

Right Half
Make 12.

6. Sew left and right halves together to complete a Heart block.

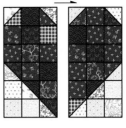

Make 12.

7. Join 6 light strips together to make a strip set. Make 3 strip sets. From the strip sets, cut 24 segments, each 2" wide.

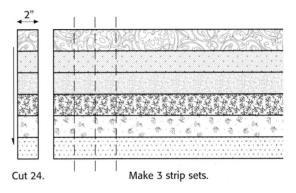

Cut 24.   Make 3 strip sets.

8. Join 4 light strips together to make a strip set. Make 5 strip sets. From the strip sets, cut 48 segments, each 2" wide.

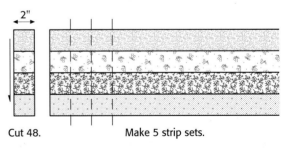

Cut 48.   Make 5 strip sets.

9. Sew a 6-square segment to opposite sides of a Heart block.

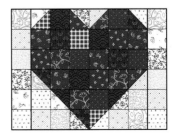

10. Join two 4-square segments to make an 8-square segment and add these to the top and bottom edges of a Heart block.

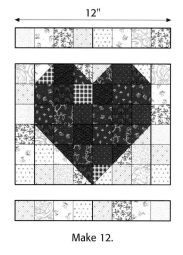

12"

Make 12.

AJJEMBLING THE QUILT

Arrange and sew the blocks into 4 rows of 3 blocks each. Join the rows.

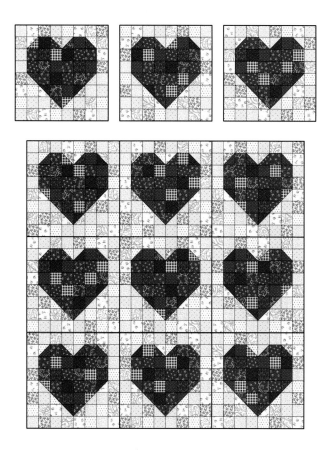

ADDING THE BORDER

1. Join 8 light 6½" squares for each of 4 borders. Sew a border to opposite sides of the quilt, then to the top and bottom edges.

2. Referring to "Bias-Strip Appliqué" on page 19, make approximately 120" of bias tubes for the vine. Referring to the color photo on page 91, appliqué a vine to 2 opposite corners of the quilt, and then add the leaves and birds.

FINIJHING THE QUILT

1. Layer the quilt top with batting and backing; baste and quilt as desired. *Quilting suggestion: Quilt a concentric heart pattern inside each heart. Stipple-quilt the sashing and borders.*

2. Referring to "Bias Binding" on page 107, cut and piece approximately 230" of bias binding and bind the edges of the quilt.

3. Using template 2 (page 95), make 18 yo-yo flowers. Attach the yo-yo flowers to the vine and secure with a knot. Stitch a button in the center of each yo-yo flower.

Turn under ¼". →

Wrong side of circle

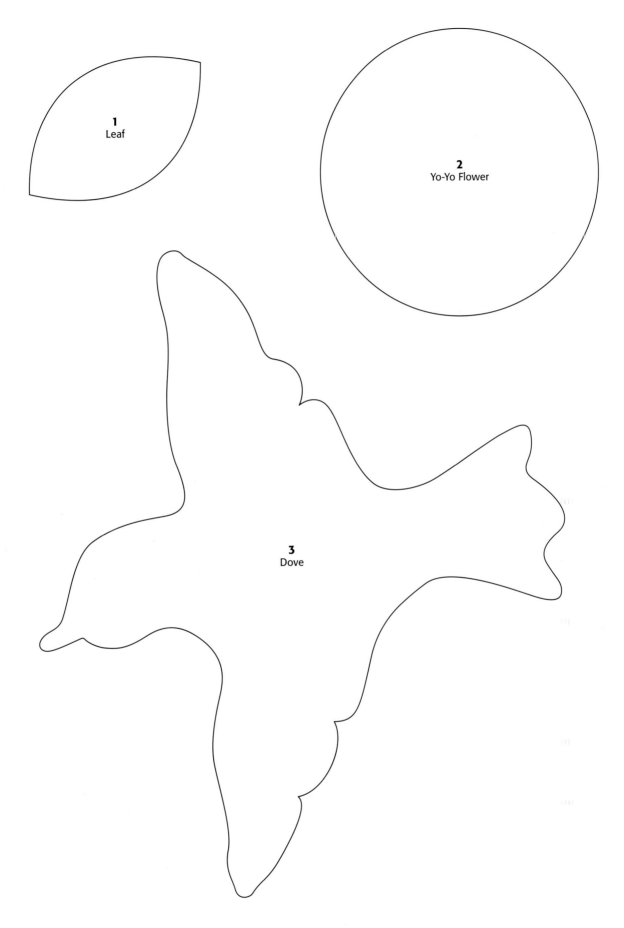

1
Leaf

2
Yo-Yo Flower

3
Dove

LAND OF LIBERTY

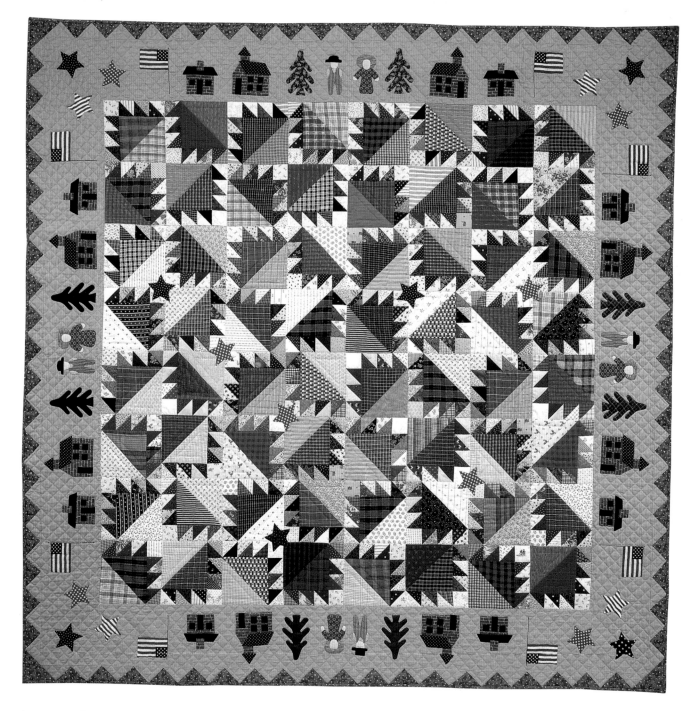

LAND OF LIBERTY BY NANCY J. MARTIN, 2001, WOODINVILLE, WASHINGTON, 84½" x 84½".
QUILTED BY ALVINA NELSON, SALINA, KANSAS.

THIS EXUBERANT *quilt, full of plaids and stripes, makes the perfect center for a border with appliquéd folk art. An appliqué border of this type is a great frame for a scrappy quilt. The border can be appliquéd and then added to the quilt, making the project portable. The stars are added after the borders are mitered.*

MATERIALS

Yardage is based on 42"-wide fabric.

- ⅓ yd. *each* of 16 assorted light prints for blocks*
- ¼ yd. *each* of 16 assorted dark prints for blocks*
- 2⅝ yds. tan check for inner and pieced borders
- ½ yd. dark blue print for pieced border
- ¼ yd. red brick print for buildings
- ¼ yd. total of assorted green prints for trees
- 2 fat eighths of assorted black prints for house details, church details, and hat
- 1 fat eighth of red print for dress
- 1 fat eighth of blue stripe for overalls
- 1 fat eighth of skin-colored solid for figures
- 1 fat eighth of red check for shirt
- 1 fat eighth of tan print for bonnet
- 8 yds. fabric for backing
- 89" x 89" piece of backing
- 8 small flags for appliqué or printed fabric with flags
- Black embroidery floss for flagpoles
- Bias Square ruler to cut bias squares

Select a wide variety of stripes, checks, plaids, shirtings, and patriotic prints with both light and dark backgrounds.

CUTTING

All measurements include ¼"-wide seam allowances.

From *each* of the 16 assorted light prints, cut:
- 2 squares, 6⅞" x 6⅞" (32 total); cut once diagonally to yield 64 triangles
- 3 squares, 8" x 8" (48 total)
- 4 squares, 2½" x 2½" (64 total)

From *each* of the 16 assorted dark prints, cut:
- 2 squares, 6⅞" x 6⅞" (32 total); cut once diagonally to yield 64 triangles
- 3 squares, 8" x 8" (48 total)

From the lengthwise grain of the tan check, cut:
- 4 strips, 8½" x 85"
- 20 squares, 5¼" x 5¼"; cut twice diagonally to yield 80 triangles

From the dark blue print, cut:
- 21 squares, 5¼" x 5¼"; cut twice diagonally to yield 84 triangles

MAKING THE BLOCKS

1. Pair each 8" light square with an 8" dark square, right sides up. Referring to "Bias Squares" on page 16, cut and piece 2½"-wide strips, and then cut 384 bias squares, 2½" x 2½".

Cut 384.

2. Sew a dark 6⅞" triangle to a light 6⅞" triangle.

Make 64.

3. Choosing fabrics randomly, join 6 bias squares, 1 light 2½" square, and 1 pieced-triangle square to make a block.

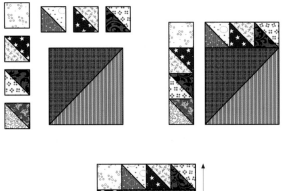

8"

Make 64.

ASSEMBLING THE QUILT

1. Arrange and sew the blocks into 8 rows of 8 blocks each, rotating the blocks as needed to form the design. Join the rows.

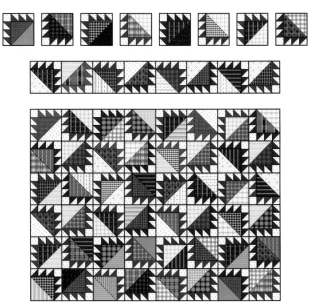

2. Refer to the quilt photo on page 96. Use the template on page 100 to cut and appliqué 7 stars randomly across the quilt top. Use a variety of fabrics.

ADDING THE BORDERS

1. Cut appliqués as indicated on the pattern pieces on pages 100 and 101.

2. Fold each 8½"-wide tan inner border in half lengthwise and crease to mark the center.

3. Using your favorite method, stitch the appliqué pieces to each inner border as shown above except for the stars in the corners, which will be added later.

4. For the flags, I cut pieces from printed fabric, pressed raw edges under ¼", and appliquéd in place.

   NOTE: *If you purchased small flags, you won't need to turn under the edges before appliquéing them.*

   Using an outline stitch, embroider the flagpoles with 2 strands of embroidery floss.

Outline stitch the flagpole.

Outline Stitch

5. Referring to "Borders with Mitered Corners" on page 104, sew the inner borders to the quilt and miter the corners.

6. Appliqué 3 stars on each mitered corner.

7. Join 21 dark blue 5¼" triangles and 20 tan check 5¼" triangles to make each of 4 pieced borders.

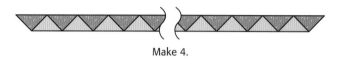

Make 4.

8. Referring to the color photo on page 96, sew the pieced borders to the quilt top and miter the corners as for the inner border.

FINISHING THE QUILT

1. Layer the quilt top with batting and backing; baste and quilt as desired. *Quilting suggestion:* Quilt the bias squares in the ditch; then quilt ½" inside each of the large triangles. Outline quilt the stars and all of the objects in the borders, including their details. Quilt a ½" diagonal grid in the tan border up to the blue triangles. Quilt the outer blue triangles in the ditch.

2. Referring to "Bias Binding" on page 107, cut and piece approximately 350" of bias binding and bind the edges of the quilt.

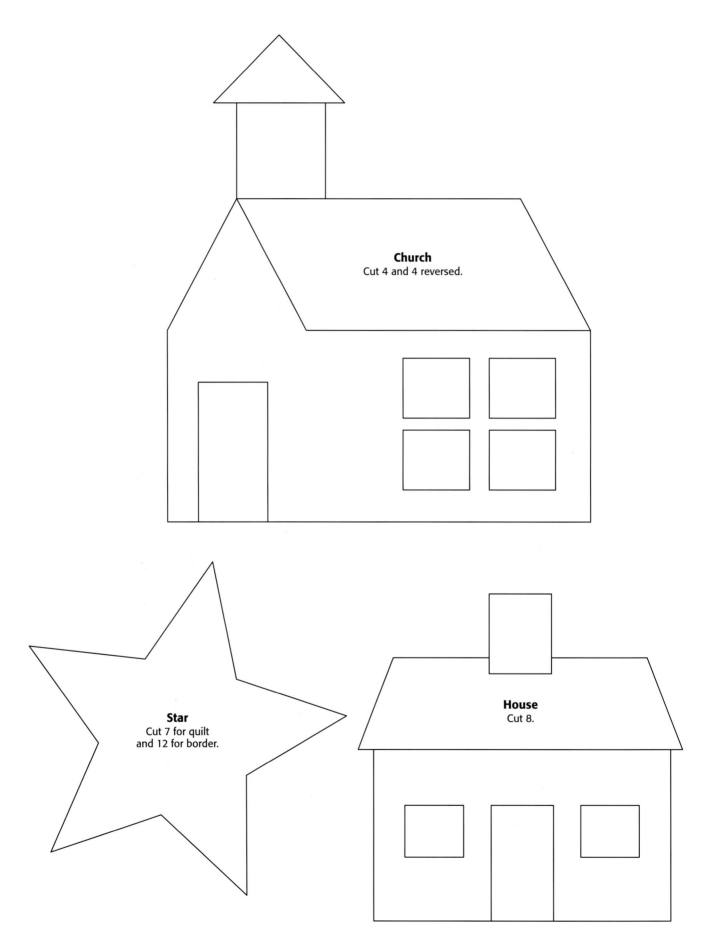

Church
Cut 4 and 4 reversed.

Star
Cut 7 for quilt
and 12 for border.

House
Cut 8.

Tree
Cut 8.

Man
Cut 4.

Woman
Cut 4.

FINISHING

AREFUL FINISHING techniques will add the final touch to your quilt top. Here are the steps that I follow to finish my quilts; they include instructions for the all-important hanging sleeve and label.

ADDING BORDERS

To make sure the border lies flat once it is sewn to the quilt top, it's important to take a few preliminary steps. To begin, straighten the edge of your quilt top before adding the borders.

Next, to find the correct measurement for borders, always measure through the center of the quilt, not at the outside edges. This ensures that the borders are of equal length on opposite sides of the quilt and brings the outer edges in line with the center dimension if discrepancies exist. Otherwise, your quilt might not be square due to minor piecing variations and/or stretching that occurred while you worked with the pieces. If there is a large difference between the two sides, it's better to go back and correct the source of the problem rather than try to make the border fit and end up with a distorted quilt.

Borders are commonly cut along the crosswise grain and seamed where extra length is needed. The seam will be strong and less noticeable if it's pieced on an angle. You may need additional fabric to do so.

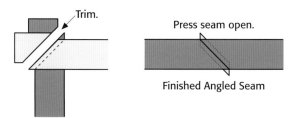

Borders cut from the lengthwise grain of fabric require extra yardage, but seaming to achieve the required length is not necessary.

Borders with Straight-Cut Corners

1. Measure the length of the quilt at the center. Cut 2 borders to this measurement, piecing as necessary.

Measure center of
quilt, top to bottom.

2. Mark the centers of the borders and the quilt top. Pin the borders to the sides of the quilt, matching the centers and ends and easing or slightly stretching the quilt to fit the border as necessary.

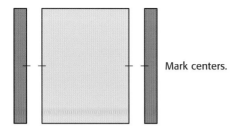

Mark centers.

3. Sew the side borders in place and press the seams toward the border.

4. Measure the center width of the quilt, including the side borders, to determine the length of the top and bottom borders. Cut 2 borders to this measurement, piecing strips as necessary. Mark the centers of the borders and the quilt top. Pin the borders to the top and bottom of the quilt top, easing or slightly stretching the quilt to fit as necessary.

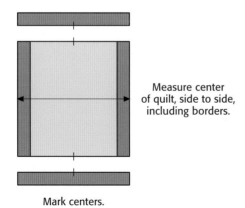

Measure center of quilt, side to side, including borders.

Mark centers.

5. Sew the top and bottom borders in place and press the seams toward the border.

Borders with Corner Squares

1. Measure the width and length of the quilt top through the center. Cut borders to those measurements, piecing as necessary.

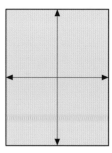

2. Mark the center of the quilt edges and the borders. Pin the side borders to opposite sides of the quilt top, matching the centers and ends and easing as necessary; stitch. Press the seams toward the border.

3. Cut corner squares of the required size, which is the cut width of the borders. Sew one corner square to each end of the remaining 2 borders; press the seams toward the borders. Pin the borders to the top and bottom edges of the quilt top. Match centers, seams, and ends, easing as necessary; stitch. Press the seams toward the border.

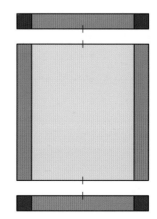

Borders with Mitered Corners

Mitered borders have a diagonal seam where the borders meet in the corners. If your quilt has multiple borders, sew the individual strips together and treat the resulting unit as a single border.

1. First estimate the finished outside dimensions of your quilt, including borders. Borders should be cut to this length plus at least ½" for seam allowances. Add 2" to 3" to be safer and to give some leeway.

2. Mark the center of the quilt edges and the borders.

3. Measure the length and width of the quilt top across the center.

4. Place a pin at each end of the side borders to mark the length of the quilt top. Repeat with the top and bottom borders.

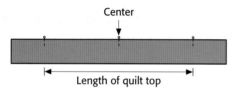

5. Pin the borders to the quilt top, matching the centers. Line up the pins at either end of the border with the quilt edges. Stitch, beginning and ending the stitching ¼" from the raw edges of the quilt top. Repeat with the remaining borders.

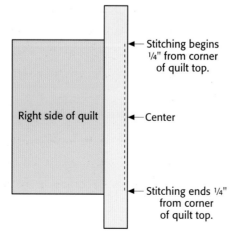

6. Lay the first corner to be mitered on the ironing board. Fold under one border at a 45° angle to the other. Press and pin.

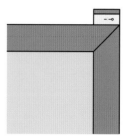

7. Fold the quilt with right sides together, lining up the edges of the border. If necessary, use a ruler and pencil to draw a line on the crease to make the line more visible. Stitch on the pressed crease, sewing from the corner to the outside edges.

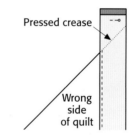

8. Press the seam open and trim the excess from the borders, leaving a ¼"-wide seam allowance.

9. Repeat with the remaining corners.

BACKING

For most quilts larger than crib size, you'll need to piece the backing from two or more strips of fabric if you use 42"-wide fabric. Seams can run horizontally (crosswise join) or vertically (lengthwise join) in a pieced backing as long as the fabric isn't a directional print. Avoid the temptation to use a bedsheet for a backing as it's difficult to quilt through.

Cut backing 3" to 4" larger than the quilt top all around. Be sure to trim away the selvages where pieces are joined. If you plan to hang your quilt, you'll need to put a sleeve or rod pocket on the back of the quilt (see page 109). Purchase extra backing fabric so that the sleeve and the backing match.

BATTING

There are many types of batting available. Select a high-loft batting for a bed quilt that you want to look puffy. Lightweight battings are fine for baby quilts or wall hangings. A lightweight batting is easier to quilt through and shows the quilting design well. It also resembles antique quilts, giving an old-fashioned look.

Polyester batting works well, doesn't shift after washing, and is easy to quilt through. It comes in lightweight and regular lofts as well as in a fat batting for comforters.

Cotton batting is a good choice if you are quilting an old quilt top. Most cotton batting must be quilted with stitches no more than 2" apart. There are, however, several new cotton battings available that may be quilted up to 8" apart. Be sure to read the manufacturer's directions to determine the type of batting you have.

LAYERING AND BASTING

Open a package of batting and smooth it out flat. Allow the batting to rest in this position for at least twenty-four hours. Cut the backing 3" to 4" larger than the quilt top all around. Press the backing so that all seams are flat and the fold lines have been removed.

A large dining-room table, Ping-Pong table, or two large folding tables pushed together make an ideal work surface on which to prepare your quilt. Use a table pad to protect your dining-room table. The floor is not a good choice for layering your quilt. It requires too much bending, and the layers can easily shift or be disturbed.

1. Place the backing on the table with the wrong side of the fabric facing up. If the table is large enough, you may want to tape the backing down with masking tape. Spread your batting over the backing, centering it, and smooth out any remaining folds.

2. Center the freshly pressed and marked quilt top, right side up, over these 2 layers. Check all 4 sides to make sure there is adequate batting and backing. Stretch the backing to make sure it's still smooth.

3. The basting method you use depends on whether you'll quilt by hand or by machine. Thread basting is generally used for hand quilting, while safety-pin basting is used for machine quilting.

Thread Basting

Starting in the middle of the quilt top, baste the three layers together with straight pins while gently smoothing out the fullness to the sides and corners. Take care not to distort the straight lines of the quilt design and the borders.

After pinning, baste the layers together with a needle and light-colored thread. (Dark-colored thread may bleed onto the quilt.) Start in the middle and make a line of long stitches to each corner to form a large X.

Continue basting in a grid of parallel lines 6" to 8" apart. Finish with a row of basting around the outside edges. Quilts that are to be quilted with a hoop or on your lap require more basting than those quilted on a frame because they will be handled more. After basting, remove the pins. Now you are ready to quilt.

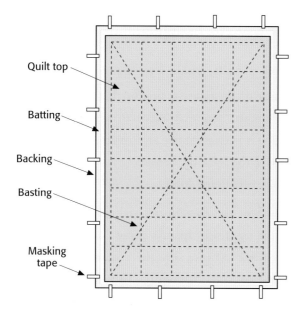

Quilt top

Batting

Backing

Basting

Masking tape

Pin Basting

A quick way to baste a quilt top for machine quilting is with size 2 safety pins. They are large enough to catch all three layers but not so large that they snag fine fabric. Begin pinning in the center and work out toward the edges. Place pins 4" to 5" apart. Baste around the outside edge with straight pins to hold everything in place.

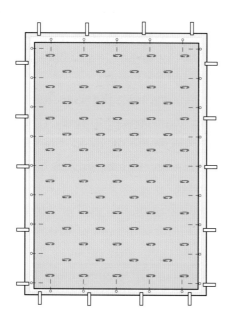

QUILTING

Hand Quilting

To quilt by hand, you need quilting thread, quilting needles, small scissors, a thimble, and perhaps a balloon or large rubber band to help grasp the needle if it gets stuck. Use a single strand of quilting thread no longer than 18". Make a small, single knot at the end of the thread. The quilting stitch is a small running stitch that goes through all three layers of the quilt. Take two, three, even four stitches at a time if you can keep them even. When crossing seams, you might find it necessary to "hunt and peck" one stitch at a time.

To begin, insert the needle in the top layer about 1" from the point you want to start stitching. Pull the needle out at the starting point and gently tug at the knot until it pops through the fabric and is buried in the batting. Make a backstitch and begin quilting. Stitches should be tiny (8 to 10 per inch is good), even, and straight; tiny will come with practice.

When you come almost to the end of the thread, make a single knot ¼" from the fabric. Take a backstitch to bury the knot in the batting. Run the thread off through the batting and out the quilt top, and then snip it off. The first and last stitches will look different from the running stitches in between. To make them less noticeable, start and stop where quilting lines cross each other or at seam joints.

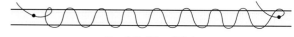

Hand-Quilting Stitch

Machine Quilting

A walking foot or even-feed foot is essential for straight-line and grid quilting and for large, simple curves. It helps feed the quilt layers through the machine without shifting or puckering. Read the machine instruction manual for special tension settings to sew through extra fabric thicknesses.

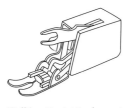

Walking Foot Attachment

If your project has intricately curved designs, use a darning foot and lower the feed dogs for free-motion quilting. Free-motion quilting allows the fabric to move freely under the foot of the sewing machine. Because the feed dogs are lowered, the stitch length is determined by the speed at which you run the machine and feed the fabric under the foot. Practice on a layer of fabric scraps until you get the feel of controlling the motion of the fabric with your hands. Run the machine fairly fast, since this makes it easier to sew smoother lines of quilting. Don't turn the fabric under the needle. Instead, guide the fabric as if it was under a stationary pencil (the needle).

Darning Foot

Stitch some free-form scribbles, zigzags, and curves. Try a heart or a star. Free-motion quilting may feel awkward at first, but with a little determination and practice, you can imitate beautiful hand-quilting designs quickly and complete a project in just a few hours.

When machine quilting, keep the spacing between quilting lines consistent over the entire project. Avoid using complex, little designs and leaving large spaces unquilted. With most battings, a 2" to 3" square is the largest area that can be left unquilted. Also, don't try to machine quilt an entire quilt in one sitting, even if it's a small quilt. Break the work into short periods, and stretch and relax your muscles regularly.

Finally, when all the quilting has been completed, remove the safety pins.

Bias Binding

My favorite quilt binding is a double-fold French binding made from bias strips. It rolls over the edges of the quilt nicely, and the two layers of fabric resist wear.

The quilt directions tell you how much fabric to purchase for binding. If, however, you enlarge your quilt, you'll need to measure the distance around your quilt and add about 10" for turning the corners and for overlapping the ends of the binding strips. Use the following chart to compute how much binding you'll need.

Length of Binding	Fabric Needed
115"	¼ yd.*
180"	⅜ yd.*
255"	½ yd.
320"	⅝ yd.
400"	¾ yd.
465"	⅞ yd.

It's a good idea to purchase ½ yard of fabric instead of ¼ or ⅜ yard so the bias strips will be longer and the binding won't have as many seams.

After quilting, trim excess batting and backing even with the edge of the quilt top. A rotary cutter and long ruler will ensure accurate straight edges. If the basting is no longer in place, baste all three layers together at the outside edges. If you are going to attach a sleeve to the back of your quilt for hanging, turn to page 109 and attach it now, before you bind the edges.

To cut bias strips:

1. Align the 45° marking of the Bias Square along the selvage and place the ruler's edge against it. Make the first cut.

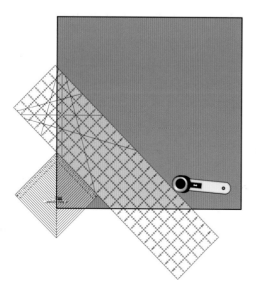

2. Measure the width of the strip (I make mine 2¼") from the cut edge of the fabric. Cut along the edge of the ruler.

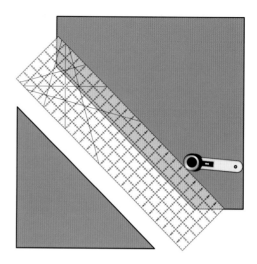

When cutting bias strips, a 24"-long ruler may be too short for some of the cuts. After making several cuts, carefully fold the fabric over itself so that the bias edges are even. Continue to cut bias strips.

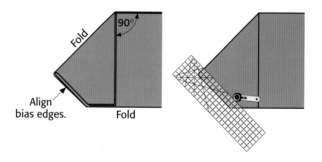

To bind the edges:

1. Stitch bias strips together, offsetting them as shown. Press the seams open.

2. Fold the strip in half lengthwise, wrong sides together, and press. Unfold the binding at one end and turn under ¼" at a 45° angle.

Fold line

3. Starting on one side of the quilt, stitch the binding to the quilt. Use a ¼"-wide seam allowance. Begin stitching 1" to 2" from the start of the binding. Stop stitching ¼" from the corner and backstitch.

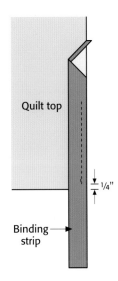

Quilt top

¼"

Binding strip

4. Turn the quilt to prepare for sewing along the next edge. Fold the binding away from the quilt, and then fold again to place the binding along the second edge of the quilt. This fold creates an angled pleat at the corner.

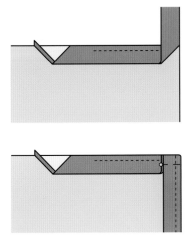

5. Stitch from the fold of the binding along the second edge of the quilt top, stopping ¼" from the corner as you did for the first corner; backstitch. Repeat the stitching and mitering process on the remaining edges and corners of the quilt.

6. When you reach the beginning of the binding, cut the end 1" longer than needed and tuck the end inside the beginning. Stitch the rest of the binding.

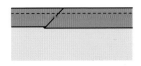

7. Turn the binding to the back side, over the raw edges of the quilt. Blindstitch in place, with the folded edge covering the row of machine stitching. At each corner, fold the binding to form a miter on the back of the quilt.

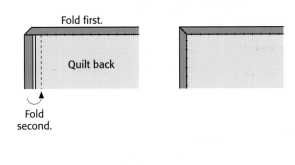

Fold first.

Quilt back

Fold second.

QUILT SLEEVES

If you plan to hang your quilt, attach a sleeve or rod pocket to the back before attaching the binding. From the leftover backing fabric, cut an 8"-wide strip of fabric equal to the width of your quilt. You may need to piece two or three strips together for larger quilts. On each end, fold over ½" and then fold ½" again. Press and stitch by machine.

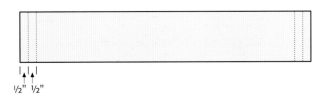

½" ½"

Fold the strip in half lengthwise, wrong sides together; baste the raw edges to the top edge on the back of your quilt. These will be secured when you sew on the binding. Your quilt should be about 1" wider than the sleeve on both sides. Make a little pleat in the sleeve to accommodate the thickness of the rod, and then slipstitch the ends and bottom edge of the sleeve to the backing fabric. This keeps the rod from being inserted next to the quilt backing.

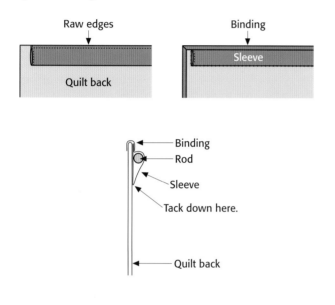

QUILT LABELS

It's a good idea to label a quilt with its name, the name and address of the maker, and the date it was made. Include the name of the quilter(s) if the quilt was quilted by a group or someone other than the maker. On an antique quilt, record all the information you know about the quilt, including where you purchased it. If the quilt is being presented to someone as a gift, also include that information.

To make a label, use a permanent-ink pen to print or legibly write all this information on a piece of muslin. Press freezer paper to the back of the muslin to stabilize it while you write. Press raw edges to the wrong side of the label. Remove the freezer paper and stitch the label securely to the lower corner of the quilt. You can also do labels in cross-stitch or embroidery.

ABOUT THE AUTHOR

NANCY J. MARTIN is a talented teacher and quiltmaker who has written more than forty books on quiltmaking. An innovator in the quilting industry, she introduced the Bias Square cutting ruler to quilters everywhere. Along with more than twenty years of teaching experience and several bestselling titles to her credit, Nancy is the founder and president of Martingale & Company, the publisher of America's Best-Loved Quilt Books®. She and her husband, Dan, enjoy living in the Pacific Northwest.

new and bestselling titles from

America's Best-Loved Craft & Hobby Books™

America's Best-Loved Quilt Books®

NEW RELEASES
Bear's Paw Plus
All through the Woods
American Quilt Classics
Amish Wall Quilts
Animal Kingdom CD-ROM
Batik Beauties
The Casual Quilter
Fantasy Floral Quilts
Fast Fusible Quilts
Friendship Blocks
From the Heart
Log Cabin Fever
Machine-Stitched Cathedral Stars
Magical Hexagons
Potting Shed Patchwork
Quilts from Larkspur Farm
Repliqué Quilts
Successful Scrap Quilts
   from Simple Rectangles

APPLIQUÉ
Artful Album Quilts
Artful Appliqué
Colonial Appliqué
Red and Green: An Appliqué Tradition
Rose Sampler Supreme

BABY QUILTS
Easy Paper-Pieced Baby Quilts
Even More Quilts for Baby: Easy as ABC
More Quilts for Baby: Easy as ABC
Play Quilts
The Quilted Nursery
Quilts for Baby: Easy as ABC

HOLIDAY QUILTS
Christmas at That Patchwork Place
Holiday Collage Quilts
Paper Piece a Merry Christmas
A Snowman's Family Album Quilt
Welcome to the North Pole

LEARNING TO QUILT
Basic Quiltmaking Techniques for:
   Borders and Bindings
   Divided Circles
   Hand Appliqué
   Machine Appliqué
   Strip Piecing
The Joy of Quilting
The Simple Joys of Quilting
Your First Quilt Book (or it should be!)

PAPER PIECING
50 Fabulous Paper-Pieced Stars
For the Birds
Paper Piece a Flower Garden
Paper-Pieced Bed Quilts
Paper-Pieced Curves
A Quilter's Ark
Show Me How to Paper Piece

ROTARY CUTTING
101 Fabulous Rotary-Cut Quilts
365 Quilt Blocks a Year Perpetual Calendar
Around the Block Again
Biblical Blocks
Creating Quilts with Simple Shapes
Flannel Quilts
More Fat Quarter Quilts
More Quick Watercolor Quilts
Razzle Dazzle Quilts

SCRAP QUILTS
Nickel Quilts
Scrap Frenzy
Scrappy Duos
Spectacular Scraps

CRAFTS
The Art of Stenciling
Baby Dolls and Their Clothes
Creating with Paint
The Decorated Kitchen
The Decorated Porch
A Handcrafted Christmas
Painted Chairs
Sassy Cats

KNITTING & CROCHET
Too Cute!
Clever Knits
Crochet for Babies and Toddlers
Crocheted Sweaters
Fair Isle Sweaters Simplified
Irresistible Knits
Knit It Your Way
Knitted Shawls, Stoles, and Scarves
Knitted Sweaters for Every Season
Knitting with Novelty Yarns
Paintbox Knits
Simply Beautiful Sweaters
Simply Beautiful Sweaters for Men
The Ultimate Knitter's Guide

Our books are available at bookstores and your favorite craft, fabric and yarn retailers. If you don't see the title you're looking for, visit us at www.martingale-pub.com or contact us at:

1-800-426-3126

International: 1-425-483-3313

Fax: 1-425-486-7596

E-mail: info@martingale-pub.com

For more information and a full list of our titles, visit our
Web site or call for a free catalog.